Photographing
PEOPLE
& PLACES

WINDWARD

Editor Keith Faulkner
Art Editor Edward Pitcher
Production Richard Churchill

Windward
an imprint owned by WH Smith & Son Limited
Registered No 237811 England
Trading as WHS Distributors,
St John's House, East Street, Leicester, LE1 6NE

© Marshall Cavendish Limited 1985

Introduction

Every subject the photographer approaches needs individual treatment. There are techniques and tricks which can turn any photograph into a picture to be proud of.

PHOTOGRAPHING PEOPLE & PLACES covers a wide range of subjects, and shows you how different photographers have tackled the problems. The emphasis is on getting out and taking pictures and, although there is a wealth of technical advice, it is the picture that matters.

The work of many top photographers is used to illustrate the wide ranging subjects, from photographing your baby to capturing the magic of a snow-covered landscape. The beautiful pictures and informative text will show you that there is much more to creative photography than simply pressing the button.

Many great photographers have obtained stunning results with the simplest equipment. So, even if your camera case does not contain the latest in sophisticated technology, PHOTOGRAPHING PEOPLE & PLACES will help you improve your pictures and get even more enjoyment and satisfaction from your camera.

Contents

Chapter 1
Photographing children
Snap time at playtime

Trying to capture children on film can be one of the most rewarding of all photographic activities, but it can also be frustrating and exasperating. Persuading a lively child to sit still and pose properly is virtually impossible. Even if you succeed, the chances are that the result will be disappointing. Nearly all the best photographs of children are candid and informal, capturing fleeting smiles or tears, a moment funny or touching, memorable or endearing.

Whether you want to photograph your own or someone else's children, one of the best approaches is to have a long informal session with the child, taking pictures as they present themselves. Be patient and let the child get used to the camera and always be prepared to waste a little film. But above all make sure the child is occupied and happy—a bored child is rarely photogenic.

Find a location where there is plenty of light available—with the unpredictable behaviour of a young child, you need a fast shutter speed and narrow apertures to keep the picture sharp—and set up or wait for situations in which you know the child responds. Your choice depends very much on the individual child. You could give toddlers their favourite toys in the lighest room in the house or photo-graph them outdoors: in the garden, by the sandpit or splashing in the paddling pool. With older children, outdoor locations with plenty of scope for bois-terous games may provide the best results.

There is no need to dress children up in their best clothes or scrub their faces. Clean children are rarely any more photogenic and are probably so un-comfortable that it is impossible to get anything more appealing than a forced smile. Even if they look less angelic, children are usually more photogenic when running about freely in their everyday clothes—grubby knees, socks falling down and all.

The best opportunities for photo-graphing children occur when they are at their most expressive or at ease: climbing trees, in the playground or on the football pitch, or when they are experiencing something new. The first time they see snow, for instance, or a first encounter with small farm animals can provoke some fascinating reactions.

Record their moments of frustration, irritation and tears as well as moments caught unawares around the house, reading by the fire or staring moodily

Smile please *To get an unusual shot, give the child something to play with and then wait for the right moment*

Burnt out wreck *To photograph children in their element you have to look for good locations, like this derelict site*

If you do not have children of your own or wish to extend your range of opportunities for photographing them, look for good locations where children will congregate. Playgrounds, parks, streets, housing estates and derelict sites are all common places for children to gather. Cameras can provoke a good deal of hampering curiosity so some photographers prefer to shoot from a distance with a long lens. But if children do spot you taking pictures secretly it may well ruin your chances of achieving any kind of rapport with them, or of obtaining any decent pictures. One way to avoid this is to let them see you with your camera, answer their questions and explain that you want to take pictures of them playing naturally. There may be some laughter and derision, but with a little persuasion, they will probably oblige. Children are less bothered about their image than adults, and once they have overcome the novelty of being photographed they will return to their games, leaving you free to take pictures. The advantage of this approach is that children have a natural tendency to put on a performance anyway. Once they know you might be photographing them, their actions may be slightly more exaggerated.

Remember when taking this sort of shot, however, that some people may disapprove of your activities, particularly if young children are involved. It is probably advisable to approach them
(continued on page 10)

Playing with fire *Children often seem to be more at ease when they are outdoors, so the garden is a good location*

Out in the street *At the sight of cameras children usually put on a performance so all their gestures become exaggerated*

out of the window. Make the most of their natural desire to show and express their feelings and be ready to capture those moments on film.

Photographing children well is less about technical knowhow and careful planning than the ability to recognize a potential picture and press the shutter at just the right moment. Planning your session rigidly can even be a disadvantage. It is easy to become so frustrated when planned shots fail to appear in the viewfinder or to become so engrossed in obtaining one particular shot that you miss all the fresh new moments that happen in the meanwhile.

Look for moments that are slightly unusual and do not always opt for the obvious shots. A birthday party is a good theme, but there are many delightful moments besides traditional highlights such as blowing out the candles. A shot of smaller children trying to cope with a large slice of sticky cake, or a crying child in a temper, might be far more memorable. The secret is to wait and be patient. Children often look their best as soon as the camera is put down, so keep it to hand for as long as you have film.

through another adult familiar to them.

Both early morning and later afternoon are probably the best times to photograph children. Out of doors the sun is low, giving form and modelling to the subject as well as warmer tones. Backlighting helps to soften the outline and rings the head with light, giving a dreamy, glowing quality that can make a mischievous child look innocent.

Choice of background is an important aspect of child photography. Unless it is particularly relevant to the picture keep it simple or throw it completely out of focus by using a large aperture.

If you are photographing children on the move, you can suggest movement in your pictures by careful choice of shutter speed. Simply select a speed which is too slow to freeze the action, or choose to blur the background slightly by panning the camera with the moving child, at a speed of around 1/30 second.

Experiment with viewpoint too. Try shooting some of the pictures from a kneeling position—the child's eye view. Shooting from this lower angle produces pictures which give the child a very dynamic quality.

Formal portraits

Although they often look forced and unnatural, formal portraits of children can be attractive and appealing.

The setting should detract as little

On the beach *Viewpoint is important in child photography and this shot benefits from being taken at the child's level*

Mud pie *One of the biggest challenges is to take photographs which offer a glimpse into the private world of children*

as possible from the child's face. Avoid patterns and stick to plain, bright clothes and an uncluttered background.

In a portrait, it is as important to emphasize character as physical details, so try to evoke a response from your sitter that typifies their character. It might be the appealing sidelong look they give when they want something special, or the way they throw back their head when giggling—so find out something about your subject beforehand.

When working with children in this kind of situation, be polite, firm and precise in your direction and they will respond as well as most adults. Their span of concentration is shorter, however, so be well prepared to work fast. To avoid wasting time, take all meter readings before the child comes on the scene by recruiting an adult as 'stand in'. Have the camera set and loaded, and have more film ready. If your child simply does not want to cooperate it is best to leave the session to another day.

To take attractive natural pictures of children, you do not need a lot of expensive equipment or ideal weather conditions. Imagination and a couple of lively children who are not afraid to show their feelings and natural emotions in front of the camera are the best ingredients. Most of all, you need to be able to recognize a good moment to press the shutter—and a lot of energy.

Children at school

As a subject, children at school offers plenty of scope for action shots, portrait studies and candids. But opportunities come and go quickly and much depends on your approach

School can seem a closed world to adults, and few parents think of it as a natural place for photography. It does, however, take a major place in children's lives for many years, and is inevitably one of the strongest influences on the way they will think, feel and act. If you have a son or daughter yourself, and are interested in recording the incidents and changes of childhood, the school years are an essential element to be included. Even if your interest is less personal and you do not have children of your own, school can be a fascinating and varied location for photography—a separate society from your own that offers plenty of opportunities for candid photography.

In general, children are easy subjects, but when they are at school much depends on the situation. The school timetable dictates your opportunities, and the classroom, for example, needs a different approach from the playground. Inevitably, there will be restrictions on

Relay race *Using a telephoto lens and framing closely emphasizes the tension of the children waiting for their turn*

Group *Try shooting children when they are at their most relaxed, even if they are playing up to the camera*

will be, and look for a position that will give you a good view of this important part of the field. Most school sports are played on fairly unsophisticated pitches, without stands and other high points that would give you an overall view, so you will probably have to photograph at ground level. Spectators behind the children playing can make a confusing background, but this can usually be kept out of focus and less distracting by using a long focus lens at full aperture.

Before the start, consider a shot of the whole team. A straightforward group portrait is not a difficult photographic assignment, and needs organization rather than artistry, yet will certainly give a lot of pleasure to all the children. If the game to follow is an important one, the attentions of a photographer will probably also give your child's team a valuable psychological advantage. Because a group portrait has a formal purpose, you must be in control of the situation for the few minutes it will take. Nothing spoils the success of such shots

Classroom *Once the children are used to your presence, keep your eyes open for spontaneous expressions*

Tray *Using a wide angle lens with care, you can extend the foreground and keep everything in focus*

where and when you can take photographs, depending on the particular school and the attitude of the teaching staff. On a few days in the school year, such as sports or open day, there are no problems of permission—parents are welcome to photograph their children. At other times, it is advisable to approach the senior teacher, explain what you want to do, and ask for cooperation. Without permission, of course, you can go no further. If you are likely to meet resistance, offer in advance a set of your photographs to the school. Another argument that you can use in your favour is to propose a class project out of the photography—involving the children in planning and taking the pictures.

Another reason for having the school's cooperation is that it is vital to spend as long as possible with a single group of children, for it does take some time for them to lose their self-conscious awareness of the camera. Infants are generally more rewarding in this respect, although they may be less cooperative to start with. Quite quickly, they will become distracted, however, and will forget completely about the presence of the camera.

One of the simplest occasions to photograph is a regular sports fixture, such as a Saturday afternoon football game with another school. Here you have the opportunity for action photography, with plenty of movement and interest. A 35 mm SLR and a moderately long focus lens—around 150 mm or 200 mm—is ideal for most events like this. From the beginning of the game, try to find out where the areas of the greatest action

as much as indecision and time wasting on the part of the photographer.

Keep the group compact rather than widely spread, as this will help fill the picture frame. You can do this by arranging the children in two or more rows for instance, with one standing, one kneeling and one sitting on the grass. Unfortunately, chairs are hardly ever available at school sports grounds. If there are a large number of children and many will have to stand, place the taller ones behind, and set up the rows so that every face can be seen. In fact, the one important rule in group shots is to compose for the faces—keep the camera high for the same reason.

The more children there are in the shot, the greater the chance that one will blink, look away at something more interesting, grimace or in some other creative way spoil the shot. To cover yourself, take several shots in quick succession. Direct the children's attention to yourself and the camera by telling them when you are about to release the shutter—in a formal portrait like this, it matters less that the occasional expression appears a little wooden than that the whole group is concentrating. Finally, always take a group shot before the game, not after. When it is over, the children will be tired and dirty, and one member at least will already have made a run for the changing rooms.

Because you are almost certain to be besieged for copies of the photograph, colour negative film is best—prints from colour transparencies are of poorer quality and are usually more expensive. This choice of film type applies to many other school photography situations.

The major occasions, such as sports day or school concerts, are more elaborate affairs, and generally offer several good opportunities for photography, particularly if they are outdoor events. As with most situations that involve children, however, you have to be able to work quickly. When taking informal shots, for example, the right moment for a picture may come and go

Chinese playtime
A high viewpoint lends playground shots more interest **Painting** *Photograph children when they are busy, and try to include some of their work* **On the grass** *A telephoto isolates these two against the grass*

13

in an instant, and even with posed, formal photographs you are likely to lose the attention of your subjects if you are uncertain of the exposure and have to fumble with the camera settings. This is the time when an automatic camera is really useful.

To be prepared for as many opportunities as possible, make a mental list of the types of shot you are likely to find. On a typical sports day, for example, subjects will not just include the events themselves. You can use the qualifying heats to look around and discover the best camera position. Try concentrating on approaches other than the obvious action shots—include close-ups of the participants, studies of the preparations behind the scenes, the reactions of the spectators, parents with children and finally the excitement of the prize giving.

Indoor occasions generally involve more technical problems, and may require the use of fast film, say ASA 400, or portable flash. School outings are other special events worth following, but the photographic possibilities will depend on the particular excursion.

For the more regular, day-to-day school activities, you will need to enlist the support of the teachers. This is especially true if you want natural and candid shots, for you will need to be around long enough for the novelty to wear off with the children. This might take the best part of a day, and then only if you try to keep yourself out of their attention. For informal pictures, the two locations are the playground and the classrooom, the playground being, on the whole, the easier.

For candid photography, the playground is unrivalled. One approach is to stay at the edge and use a long focus lens. You will find that there are several children concentrating so hard on their activities that you will go unnoticed. Look out for close-ups of interesting expressions, full-figure shots of children absorbed in some activity, and groups playing games.

If, on the other hand, you are prepared to become involved yourself, move in closer with a standard 50 mm or wide-angle lens. You can expect the types of attitude, expression and activity to be different. In this case, let the children show you what interests them—it is a great opportunity for them to show off,

and you can take advantage of it.

By choosing the approach of involvement you have, in effect, entered the playground world, and so to some extent you will have to follow the tide of the children's interests. If a group of children set themselves up for an impromptu portrait, oblige them. Having taken the shot, however, you can expect to be besieged by other requests. Carry plenty of film and work quickly.

In the classroom, the atmosphere will be more formal and your presence is likely to be more disruptive, so the best approach is to have the teacher introduce you without delay. Explain what kind of photographs you want to take, and why, and then sit down quietly, out of the way, until the children have lost interest in you. For natural, unposed shots of the children at work, use available light rather than flash. This will require high-speed film and, if possible, a quiet camera.

Classes in practical subjects, such as art, woodwork and cooking will give you the most interesting opportunities. Infant schools often provide more varied activities such as singing and dancing, although older children concentrating on their work in a science laboratory, for example, can produce very good pictures. Scientific equipment can add visual interest and it is very effective to show just what the child is working on, thus telling a story with your pictures.

In the same way, it is often a good idea

Boys in grey *A wide angle lens from a high angle makes the most of a small and cluttered classroom*

School in the sun *If you can work unobtrusively, you may get some very natural and candid group shots*

African child *You can take time to make a carefully composed picture while a child is concentrating hard*

Angels *School theatre productions are always good sources of material. Use fast film if the lighting is dim*

to include a blackboard in the shot. This establishes the context of the studying in progress—perhaps the blackboard will show mathematical problems or diagrams or a list of the characters in a play. The person looking at your photographs will immediately become more interested in the children and identify with them if he or she knows what they are studying. And do not forget the teacher. Activities probably make the best subjects for classroom pictures but interactions between teacher and children can also produce good shots.

If you become involved with the school, you will almost certainly find yourself being enlisted to help, perhaps with the setting up of the school darkroom. To start with, children will just want to take pictures of each other pulling faces—but you can lead them from that to using photographs for school projects—perhaps taking portraits of members of staff or recording places around the school. If you do try a little informal coaching of the school's keener young photographers, work with small numbers.

All aspects of school life offer good opportunities, and there is sufficient variety for you to expect more than just one or two good photographs from a single session. By planning to cover a number of different events and activities, you could have the makings of a rich and interesting photographic essay.

Photographing your baby

Every proud parent wants to record those years of babyhood that seem to fly by so quickly. But photographing even the most angelic baby can present problems . . .

Lighting *George aimed to have the sun coming over Ruby's shoulder in this session so that just the edge of her face was caught by direct sunlight and there were no harsh shadows. Slight back-lighting also helped to soften the outline and ensured that George's own shadow was kept well out of the frame*

Over the months, George Wright tried to make a photographic record of Ruby as she grows. He has photographed her in many locations and in many of her changeable moods and we thought that this assignment would present few problems. But we asked George to show us what can go wrong.

George did not feel the lawn was an ideal location because light reflected from the bright green grass can give everything else a green cast. But there are a number of advantages for beginners. There is usually plenty of natural light available. The green shows up strong colours like red particularly well.

And above all, there is plenty of space for the baby to move around in without getting up to mischief.

Although it meant that Ruby sometimes had her back to the camera, she was allowed to crawl around the lawn freely and George simply waited for the right moment before pressing the shutter.

Of course, with Ruby moving around constantly, George had trouble keeping her in focus, but by carefully 'pulling the focus' adjusting the focus on the camera as Ruby moved towards him—he was able to keep pictures sharp. He could have achieved the same effect either by holding the focus and snapping the

Panning *George followed Ruby closely as she crawled across the lawn but sometimes she moved towards him . . .*

Out of focus *With a wide aperture, depth of field is restricted and it can be hard to keep a moving baby in focus*

In focus *Here George successfully 'pulled focus' as Ruby came forwards, but has not maintained a good viewpoint*

Distractions *George failed to notice the apples that seem to have spun from Ruby's ears in the picture on the right*

Watch the background *Unlike the others, this shot is not head-on and the sun illuminates Ruby's face nicely, but the dark shadow on the grass spoils it*

shutter only when Ruby was in the right place or by following her around and keeping her at the same distance all the time. Neither of these approaches seemed satisfactory. By simply holding focus from a fixed position, he would miss many potentially good shots and by moving around with the baby he encountered all sorts of other problems. Pulling the focus requires a little practice but George found it by far the best technique in this situation.

Ruby herself found the camera fascinating and kept extending sticky fingers towards the lens and she was definitely aware of being the centre of attention. So none of the pictures were unposed and candid on her part. Candid pictures are only possible if the child is completely absorbed in some other activity.

Equipment

For this assignment, George used a 105 mm lens, slightly longer than normal, to fill the frame with his subject without getting intimidatingly close. With plenty of light available, he was also able to shoot with a fairly slow, 64 ISO, film.

Of course, with Ruby moving around

Almost right *The situation was good—Ruby was close to the camera but began to clap just as George fired*

The final picture *Instead of giving up when Ruby started clapping, George waited for her to stop for an instant and then captured this delightful picture*

Simple snaps with children

Children may be natural subjects for a photograph, but sometimes they may freeze up if put into an awkward setting. Even a simple camera will produce good results if the approach is right

Professional photographers tend to use a vast array of equipment in their work but this is mainly because they need to get pictures despite many unpredictable limitations. In ordinary circumstances the most basic equipment is often perfectly adequate. To see how a professional would do on an 'amateur' assignment with amateur equipment, we asked Chris Barker to try photographing his children with just an Olympus Trip and a small Rollei flash.

'I came across several difficulties,' said Chris. 'In particular it took me some time to get used to the non-TTL viewfinder. Being used to an SLR I had a tendency to assume that because everything looked sharp, the camera was in focus. Also, the fixed wide angle lens made framing difficult and forced me to move in much closer than I would have liked. If given the choice I would certainly have used a longer lens such as a 105 mm on an SLR.'

In addition to the technical problems caused by the Trip's limitations, Chris also had more human problems with his subjects. The girls were happy to pose indefinitely but his son was a rather reluctant subject. Chris had to waste a certain amount of film, shooting a number of shots in an attempt to break the ice.

Looking around the location in which he had chosen to shoot, a friend's garden, Chris found and used a selection of props. The rose and slide were 'a bit

Double portrait *Chris had to get in very close to frame the pair tightly and in general he found the Trip's lens frustratingly wide*

Barrel *Rather than try to persuade his unwilling son to smile, Chris posed him by a convenient barrel and took this moody portrait*

Slide *The slide was too small to allow for real action shots so Chris posed the girl on top and waited for the wind to catch her hair and add life*

Swing *Using any props available to add variety to his shots, Chris set up this photo, getting the children to look over a shoulder at the peak of the action*

to use the flash on a lead, if it had been possible, as the hot-shoe mounted flash tended to give a rather flat and bland light. To make sure the exposures were correct, Chris set the aperture manually, bracketing each shot just to be on the safe side.

'Once I'd got used to the Trip it proved a very simple camera to use, allowing me to concentrate on the location, the composition and the kids. The main thing with this type of photography, though, is to work fast and not let the kids get restless—bored kids make bad photos. Given the choice I would still prefer to use a SLR with a longer lens as it gives you just that bit more flexibility and lets you use techniques like differential focusing.'

corny but effective' and the swing helped add a touch of variety with a few action shots.

Quite early on in the session Chris decided that using the sun as back-lighting, with the flash providing fill-in light, could give attractive results. First, the children, with the sun behind them, had no tendency to squint. Second, the sun made a delightful golden fringe of the children's blond hair and this could be made to stand out attractively against a dark, shady background. Nevertheless, Chris felt that he would have preferred

Boy *Trying to make the most of the location, Chris searched out pleasing bits of the garden to act as backgrounds for the children*

Rose *Though slightly corny, Chris liked this shot, feeling that the girl's pensive, almost melancholy, look rescued it from being too clichéd*

Mother and child

Whether you are taking formal portraits or candid shots, the theme of mother and child offers lots of scope for material ranging from the moment of birth right through childhood

Kenyan mother and child *Hands and arms can be used to introduce a strong line into a simple composition, and to join two subjects more closely together*

One of the great traditional themes in painting and sculpture—the portrait of mother and child—can also be a very rewarding subject for photography.

A natural time to start is when the mother is expecting. Maternity clothes are seldom flattering, however, and you can express more about the condition of pregnancy if you have the chance to photograph the mother-to-be nude. Clearly this will be easier if you are the father of the child or a close friend of the expectant mother. A woman photo-

grapher may find she has far more natural sympathy and understanding for the pregnant state. Equally, the pregnant woman may feel at ease with another woman, and so may express her feelings more clearly.

A gentle window light, especially on an overcast day when there are no

shadows, is best for emphasizing the newly rounded form of the mother-to-be. Try to take this type of picture against a plain background, since you are dealing mainly with light and form, and a cluttered background will be a distraction.

If your subject is reluctant to pose in the nude, ask her to dress in something very lightweight, and look at the silhouette effect that is produced when you backlight such clothing so that the pregnant form is contrasted with the surrounding garment. While the shape is the most important part of the photograph, do not ignore details of the body. Her hands, for instance, can be used to emphasize the increased girth, and her face, in particular, at this highly emotional time, may betray feelings of joy, on the one hand, and tiredness and discomfort, on the other.

If there are other children in the family, you can use their excitement and interest at the prospect of a new brother or sister to great effect in the picture. Again, try to use simple window light, with an additional reflector if necessary. Seat the mother in a chair, with the child at her feet feeling for the baby's movements with face or hands pressed up against the pregnant form. Make sure that you can see the child's face clearly in your picture as he or she may very suddenly break into smiles of delight as the baby's kicks are felt. It is probably best to stand back, using a telephoto lens, and frame closely.

The shape of the expectant mother changes predictably over a period of time, and you may find it interesting, particularly if you are the father, to make a monthly photographic record of these developments, concentrating on simple shape and form and framing quite closely to avoid distractions.

As the time of confinement approaches, you may consider taking some photographs of the birth itself. While a home delivery gives you a marvellous opportunity to photograph the event in the peace and quiet of a bedroom, some hospitals allow photography during a normal labour and birth, particularly if you are the father. Always ask permission first, and see if the hospital authorities will let you look at the labour ward beforehand, so that you can assess what equipment and film it would be best to use.

In the circumstances of a birth it is probably kinder not to use flash, and many hospitals would prefer that you do not, in any case. A fast black and white film will be best for this occasion, and a wide angle lens may be useful to show the mother in the context of the busy hospital labour ward, and may be essential in the more cramped delivery room if you want to show the whole scene in one shot.

Ideally, to avoid changing lenses and missing a few precious seconds, it is best to have a second camera with you, even if you have to borrow it for the day, so that you can also take some telephoto shots of the mother's face as it reveals the extremes of physical pain and intense joy as the baby arrives. At this point you will have to stand back in order not to be in the way of the delivery itself, so it may be an idea to find something to stand on, so that you still have a clear view of the birth. Always discuss with the mother the type of photographs you want to take well before labour actually begins. There may well be certain moments that she does not want to be recorded on film.

When the baby has arrived safely and is handed to the mother to hold for the first time, the nature of your subject changes dramatically. Make sure that you are ready, not only for the ecstatic moment when mother first sees the child she has been carrying for so long, but also for the time when you are no longer dealing with one person as the principal subject of the photograph, but two, each of whom is as important as the other. This may not seem so obvious at first, since most babies are red-faced, wrinkled little beings, who do not seem attractive to any but their own parents. It is up to you, as the photographer, to try to make the best portrait possible at this time, for it may be this first mother and child photograph that will be the most cherished recollection the proud parents possess of their child.

At this early stage a black and white portrait may be best if the baby is particularly red-faced, and a medium telephoto lens may be a useful way of capturing these first precious moments without being intrusive. Photographing two people together is considerably more challenging than photographing one person alone, and both composition and lighting will now need more consideration. Do not expect any expression on a newly-born baby's face, except those extremes of hunger, discomfort or sleepiness, but concentrate instead on the mother's expressions as she reacts to the demands of her new infant with love and attention. There will be plenty of time to reveal the baby's expression after a few weeks.

Watch the mother as she inspects each part of the new baby, and you may catch that delightful moment as she counts both fingers and toes, just to make sure that everything is there. Do not try to pose your subjects, or readjust their clothes or hair for this first portrait, but see instead how you can get a better viewpoint by altering your position, perhaps

Tee-shirts *If strong directional light falls on your subjects, use fill-in light or a reflector to show the subjects' faces more clearly*

Peek-a-boo *Seating a child on the mother's lap gives you the chance of a clear profile shot, and allows your subjects to interact more closely*

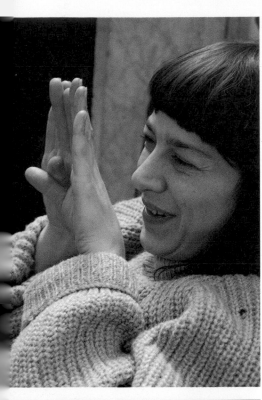

Hands *You do not have to show faces in all your shots—details can be just as effective, especially where the lighting brings out colour and texture*

using a chair to stand on to look down. In particular, do not disturb the moment when the baby first feeds. Your photographs at this stage can exploit the difference in size between mother and child. Sometimes details can express this best, for instance, a close-up of a tiny fist curled around an adult finger, or a tiny head suckling a breast which may almost equal its size.

Thai mother and child *Good images arise naturally from the harmonious form of mother and child so be prepared for candids*

The first formal photographs of mother and child are usually taken after four or five weeks have passed. There is good reason for this since, by this time, most babies are, quite simply, a lot better looking, and most mothers are too. Both have had a chance to recover from the ordeal of birth and settle into a daily routine; more importantly mother and child have had the chance to get to know

one another and established a relationship upon which you can concentrate.

One factor which will help enormously at this stage is that the baby's eyes begin to focus and look around. The mother undoubtedly will be delighted at this development which is a prelude to other facial expressions and this first important contact between mother and child is not difficult to show in your pictures. If you place mother and baby in a chair in front of a window so that the mother is holding the baby in front of her, and both faces are seen in profile for instance, the baby may gaze up into the mother's face

23

and you will be able to show how one responds to the other quite clearly.

This kind of shot benefits from a broad diffused light source from the window. Use just a white card reflector to fill in shadows because a complex lighting set-up may destroy the mood of quiet informality which exists, while flash shots may fluster the baby. In addition, the bright light generated by flash can often reflect surrounding colours on to the baby's very pale skin. For the same reason it is probably best to avoid bright backgrounds and pay careful attention to what the mother may be

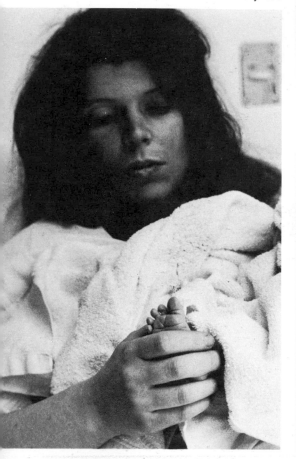

Counting toes *For the first portrait in hospital, stand back and use a telephoto lens, and you may catch an intimate moment without intruding*
Looming shadow *Shadows can play an important part in a composition. Here the shadow of a building seems to both menace and protect the couple*
On the grass *When taking candid shots, set a fast shutter to stop the action. This picture makes creative use of a dynamic shadow as a foreground, while a high angle gives an uncluttered view of the scene*

wearing which may have the same effect.

This type of composition with mother and baby in profile at a window with one face close to and responding to another usually works very well. In mother and child portraits in particular, where a successful composition depends on the happy relationship of one face to another, the position of the two heads within the frame is crucial. Neither head should dominate the picture entirely.

Generally, it is best to arrange the subjects so that the two heads fall on a diagonal, perhaps one slightly above and to the left, the other slightly below and to the right. A degree of overlap, where one head is in front of the other, creates an interesting balance of shapes within the frame as well. Occasionally pictures in which two faces are side by side can work well, but usually this arrangement needs some extra element, perhaps the subjects' arms or hands, to balance the design.

Bathtime is always a good moment for capturing mother and child together, and a transparent plastic bath avoids the need for a high angle position to include more baby and less bath. In this case, try to keep the background fairly plain and clear of the usual bathroom clutter which will only detract from your shot. Drape the offending background with bath-towels, if necessary, make sure that you can see the mother's and baby's expression clearly, and be prepared for a certain amount of movement.

The first birthday usually brings the age of mobility, and the problems for the

Pregnant mother *Soft focus works well with delicate subject material, while delicate backlighting and a pale, clear background help to soften the image*

Heads together *Faces side by side make a more interesting composition when they are at slightly different angles. Hands can be used to balance the shot*

photographer now change. Toddlers are likely to remove themselves from the picture at short notice to investigate a new toy. The best way to create a few relatively still moments for both mother and child is to encourage a game together. As the child grows up you will find this an increasingly useful way of keeping your subjects in one place and producing interesting situations.

Always be prepared to take plenty of photographs where children are concerned, partly to make sure that you catch all the unpredictable expressions and movements, and partly to get them used to the camera. The more they see it the more they are likely to return to the activities you want to photograph. If you do direct your subjects, it is important with mother and child portraits not to destroy any natural expressions, so watch carefully the way in which they behave together naturally, rather than imposing anything on them.

Mealtimes, outings and bedtime are good occasions. Always try to give a shot a little extra thought to lift the picture out the ordinary. For instance, a mother and child reading together could be viewed through a half-opened door, or from outside a window, so that the door or window provides a frame within the picture to enclose the pair and enhance the intimacy of the occasion. The window as a frame can also be used in reverse with a playful encounter in the garden photographed from inside.

25

Chapter 2
Photographing people
Portraits

The very idea of taking formal portraits fills many photographers with horror. The word 'formal' itself suggests something straightlaced and rigid, out of the Victorian era, and possibly even with clamps to hold the subject in place. Or one thinks of the portrait taken at school, where the photographer set up a standard plain background and lighting arrangement, and every child had to sit in a standard way.

Yet even in Victorian times some photographers were beginning to let their subjects 'breathe', and the portraits of well-known people taken by such photographers as Julia Margaret Cameron are far from the stylized mould. Today, there is a wider range than ever, and it is hard to tell where the formal photograph ends and the candid shot takes over.

Most formal portraits, however, are better termed 'posed' photographs. Here, the session is set up with the aim of

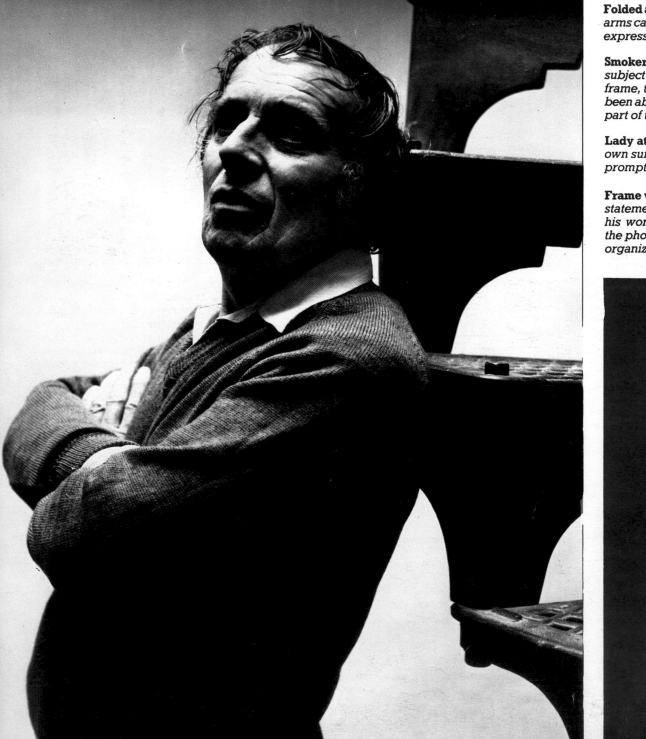

Folded arms *The position of the arms can add an extra means of expression*

Smoker *By positioning the subject's head high up in the frame, the photographer has been able to feature the hand as part of the shot*

Lady at home *The subject's own surroundings often prompt a more relaxed pose*

Frame within frame *To make a statement about the man and his work—he is an architect— the photographer created an organized, graphic shot*

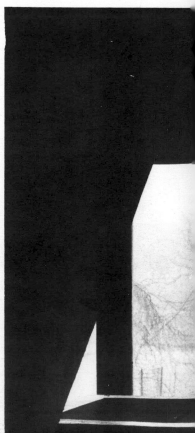

taking the subject's picture, and the subject expects to cooperate with you in order to achieve this. The traditional portrait is taken in the studio, or at least a temporary studio, but it is quite possible to take formal portraits outdoors (see pages 42 to 47) or in a room (see pages 32 to 36).

Studio photography is in many ways the hardest of all types of portrait photography—paradoxically because so much is under your control. You must attend to every part of the picture, instead of letting the background worry about itself or putting up with whatever light happens to be around at the time. For both you and the subject it is a novel

experience, which means that you must pay great attention to detail.

A professional portraitist, for example, will even wear clothes which are appropriate to the session, in cases where a stranger is to be photographed. A judge or mayor, for example, may well respond better to a photographer wearing a suit than one casually dressed, while the owner of a trendy wine bar might be the opposite.

You should also take a professional approach to the session, even when photographing a friend, in the way you set things up. It is vital to prepare the set thoroughly beforehand, so that your subject does not quickly get bored with the whole thing. You ought to have some sort of idea what kind of pictures you want before you start. This is easier in the case of friends than of strangers whose personality you have no idea of until you meet them. A true character study, rather than a simple likeness, means much more than putting your subject on the ready-lit set, however. It is important to be able to make rapid changes to the set-up during the session as the subject's personality emerges, and again this means having things ready beforehand. To start with, it is best to

well. The beginner does not have such a stock available from experience, so a useful alternative would be to collect a library of poses that you like and show them to your subject. If the pictures are good they will probably be quite keen to be photographed in such a way, and will instantly get an idea of what you want. Having established common ground, you can then explore various possibilities, developing an idea from a basic theme.

The subject's personality can be revealed in a wide variety of ways by the pose itself. There is no secret to discovering such poses—they are mostly fairly obvious. A subject who leans forward will appear aggressive, while one who leans back will appear either relaxed or submissive.

The graphic appearance of the body and clothes also have considerable effect on the viewer. Rounded shapes are soft and are often thought of as feminine, while sharp or angular patterns, with cutting eges, are aggressive or masculine. These shapes can be produced by the subject's arms or legs, often subtly. Arms, for example, may be folded across the chest to produce an angular, aggressive effect; or hands can be cupped around the face to give a pensive, possibly shy look. Including a subject's hands in a close-up shot introduces another element to what might otherwise be a rather bland picture of a face. The angle from which you take the shot can also affect appearances. Cecil Beaton, the English society photographer, often photographed women from above eye level because he said it made their faces appear heart-shaped. You can experiment with your subject by trying the same pose from above eye level, moving down as far as waist level. Given the

Truman Capote *The shape of the hat and the positioning of the subject low in the frame created this striking composition*

photograph a range of friends, experimenting with showing their characters in different ways, before tackling portraits of strangers.

The problem of assessing your subject's character is central to the success of the portrait. Different photographers have different ways of doing this. Inevitably you form snap judgements, in which case you are likely to portray the personality that the person is trying to project rather than their true inner self. Your ability to judge people and to get on with them is not the sort of thing that can be developed in any way other than by experience, however. It is safe to assume, though, that if someone dresses and behaves in either an aggressive or timid way, that they will be quite happy with portraits which reinforce those characteristics.

There are also different ways of handling the session itself. It is usually preferable to talk directly to the subject, and to get them to respond to you, rather

than to the impersonal lens of the camera. This means using a tripod, so that you are not hidden behind the camera as you speak. Having focused, take your eye away from the viewfinder and talk normally to the person. Once you have the pose looking good, you can ask them to look at the lens for a picture which you take using a cable release, without even looking through the viewfinder.

On the other hand some portraitists will virtually ignore the camera, and will bustle around attending to various details so that the subject is caught virtually off guard and does not assume a fixed pose when the cable release is pressed. This method tends to produce a rather serious portrait, since the subject has made no effort to look pleasant or interested, but it may reveal more personality than a posed shot, since the subject is less self-conscious.

When faced with your subject, often the hardest thing is actually getting the session under way. Even professional portrait photographers can have this problem, and one solution is to have a stock of poses which you know work

Man and his music *While backgrounds should usually be kept simple. there are always cases for breaking the rules*

Fashion designer *For portraits where the subject is positioned centrally, try using the surroundings as a frame*

Singer's profile *The sweeping lines formed by the arms balance the composition and give it strong, graphic qualities*

Window light
Daylight can be a very effective light source for portraiture and can also allow you to use the window itself as part of the shot

Young girl *Flash can also be used in a way that simulates daylight. Here the directional illumination has been used to bring out the texture in the wall and to cast unusual, striking shadows*

Lana Turner *This has all the elements of a classic portrait—careful lighting, composition according to the rule of thirds and the bold shapes described by the subject's limbs*

individual, rather than reveal aspects of character. In this case, extremes are undesirable. A standard rule among portrait photographers is that you should never allow the subject to look down on you. Double chins become pronounced, wrinkles sag and you find yourself confronted with distended notrils. If in doubt, therefore, you should keep your viewpoint at or above eye level, foreshortening the face. Other techniques for flattering subjects are to use diffuse, fairly frontal, lighting to soften wrinkles, and to keep the main lighting above eye level, but not so high as to produce shadowed eye sockets. Bear in mind, too, that dark skinned people often prefer to appear lighter, while a fair skinned person will usually like to appear to have a tan. Ask your subject whether they have a good side, and ignore this information at your peril!

In formal portraits, backgrounds should be kept as simple as possible—unless you have a particular interest in trying to relate the subject to his or her surroundings or interests. Generally, the best background is either a plain wall or background paper—or even an expanse of sky. Watch out for distracting

fairly long focal lengths common in portrait work, this is not as extreme as it sounds.

Other techniques used to reveal character are often aimed at helping the subject to lose self-consciousness. A profile, for example, enables them to look away from the camera, though they might find the result unflattering, as most people rarely see their profiles. Any imperfections of the profile, such as poorly shaped chins or noses, will become very obvious. To avoid this, yet still achieve a different pose, you can ask your subject to look away then look back at you. Using a rapid shutter speed or flash, take the picture when they are not quite facing you, though their eyes are looking at the camera.

For head and shoulders shots where the subject dominates the frame, there is just as much need for careful composition as with full length shots. One consideration is whether or not to frame the shot so that there is space around the edges or so the portrait fits exactly into the confines of the viewfinder. There is justification for both, depending on the effect you want to achieve. There is also a strong case for framing just a selected area—perhaps cropping out the top of the head, for instance.

There is also a need to think about whether or not the main subject should be framed centrally or to one side of the centre. General principles of composition apply just as much to portraiture as to landscape or any other type of photography, so that framing the main subject in accordance with the 'rule of thirds' is often a safe choice. Of course, though this does not have to be observed rigidly and it is a mistake to adhere strongly to a fixed set of rules.

Some portraits aim to flatter the

shadows, although, of course, it can be very effective to deliberately make a strong shadow part of the portrait.

In your search for an interesting and revealing portrait, it is a good idea to look at those taken by famous portraitists. There is often a clear style associated with each one, and with specific eras. Pictures taken in the first half of the century, for example, tended to be rather stylized and relied on strange or dramatic lighting for their originality. In the 60s, people became keen on lighting each shot with several lights—main light, fill-in, highlight (or kicklight) and maybe one or two others. This showed that the picture had been taken in a studio with plenty of facilities around. The trend since then has been towards more naturalistic photographs, often completely forsaking the studio in favour of everyday surroundings.

Photographers have tried a wide range of techniques to reveal character.

Grain, blurring, contrast, multiple exposure, double exposure, montaging and practically every other technique can be added to the armoury of lighting and poses to reveal facets of character. It is inevitable that you may repeat ideas used by others, either knowingly or unwittingly, but the vast range of human characteristics makes it possible to treat every subject differently, so that each portrait is as individual as the person it represents.

Portraits taken indoors

Portraits taken by available light indoors too often yield only simple likeness pictures. But by using its peculiarities, available light can transform portraits into telling personality studies

Available light indoors is ideal for portraiture, in which good results depend so much on a relaxed and informal atmosphere. Although outdoor lighting can clearly be more varied, and the results may be more spontaneous, you have very little control over the quality of light or the weather conditions. On the other hand, in a studio setting with artificial lights you may find that the very formality of the situation puts pressure on both model and photographer, and the results can easily appear contrived.

An ordinary interior, however, allows the subject to relax in a fairly natural environment, while allowing you some control over the illumination. This is obviously desirable when photographing portraits—and indeed many photographers who specialize in informal portraits, rather than the stylized formal pictures, prefer to use available light without resorting to flash, which can totally destroy the mood of a shot and produce unforeseen results.

At one time, photography indoors without extra lighting was regarded as an extreme approach, only to be attempted if there was no alternative. Today, improved films and lenses make it possible to take pictures indoors with few problems. Many beginners' results are poor not because of lack of light, but because they are not sufficiently aware of the nature of available light—in particular, its high contrast. Each of the possible in-

By the window *Compare this study with the others, which are two quite different character statements despite the similar indoor settings.*

Ringmaster *This colourful portrait, by clever and careful posing, tells us something about a man, who is very proud of his own image*

Quentin Crisp *Your subject need not fill the frame to make a successful portrait. The details of the room can reveal a great deal about a personality*

door light sources has its own peculiarities and uses. You may not always be able to pick and choose the light source, but if you know the type of results which each will give it is possible to achieve a wide degree of control.

When photographing people, you must think more carefully than usual what effect you are aiming for. This depends on the relationship between you and your subject, and who the picture is for. If it is for the subject, they will expect to be seen in a flattering light — or at least not unflattering. On the other hand, if the picture is for you, you may want to reveal a particular aspect of the subject's personality. Either way, the way you handle the composition and the lighting will have a profound effect on the result. Achieving either a flattering light or one which will reveal aspects of your subject's personality depends on knowing how each source of available light will appear on film.

Indoor lighting by day varies from direct sunlight pouring through a window, to diffused window lighting reflected off walls near the centre of a room. Artificial lighting may vary from the stark illumination given by a single overhead naked light bulb to the diffuse glow of wall lights. In addition, there may be movable lights such as desk lamps and lamp standards. The light on your sub-

ject can be a combination of all these, or you may be able to vary the light by turning lights off, moving them around, or drawing curtains.

Each type of light has its own characteristics. Direct sunlight indoors is the most contrasty and 'hard' of all. Sunlight streaming through large windows may seem the obvious choice of illumination. There are problems of excessive contrast, however, with the risk of large black areas. In many cases it will be preferable to diffuse the light in some way, or to use reflectors. You may, for example, hang a white bedsheet over the window to diffuse the light, or use white reflectors (newspapers or bedsheets will do) to reflect light into the shadows. This could look unnatural if overdone, since one does not expect to see large amounts of diffuse light coming from inside a room. Alternatively, a Venetian blind on the window throws patterns on to the subject, giving an unusual effect with its own value in creating a mood or helping to mould a subject.

Direct sunlighting can provide very dramatic lighting conditions, and has produced many successful portraits, both in classical art and in photography. It is, however, often tricky to handle both aesthetically and technically. Watch out for ugly shadows on the face, and use your light meter close to the subject to take readings of highlights and shadows. Your exposure should be an average between the highlights and the darkest tone you expect to show clearly with no more than about four stops between them.

Much of the drama of sunlit indoor portraits, however, stems from the way the subject is picked out in bold relief, so this approach may be worth using where the background is cluttered, if it can be kept in shadow.

On an overcast day, or when no direct sunlight is shining into the room, the light is more diffused, but still very hard and directional. The farther you move into the room the more diffused it becomes as reflections from the walls gain strength. The degree of diffuseness

Afternoon sunlight *often yields a mellow, peaceful portrait*

George Cole *The image of the actor's face was burned out during printing*

depends on many factors, such as the furnishing and wall covering, and the room's aspect—a basement with a window will have light coming mostly from the upper half of a window, while an upper storey flat will have a good deal of light on the ceiling. Such light can be quite diffuse and flattering, and is even enough to allow you to move around trying different angles, rather than forcing you and the subject to remain in more or less one spot.

Artificial lighting is often very contrasty. This can be surprising, as it is not noticeable in everyday life. Film, however, is far more susceptible than the eye to contrasts of light and dark.

A single overhead lamp, whether or not it has a shade, gives a very harsh light. This gives a stark appearance to the picture, but is very restrictive unless you want this sort of effect, which often suggests poverty or loneliness. Where more than one light is available, how-

ever, a softer effect is possible. Ideally there should be enough lighting to fill in the shadows. The most flexible results come from a movable desk light or spot. On their own, either of these will give hard lighting, but used in conjunction with other room lighting they can be helpful.

A wide range of lighting effects are therefore possible, from lighting from below to give the subject a sinister or powerful appearance to flattering diffuse light. In addition to daylight and room lighting, you may need to use white and

also have a great influence on the mood of the picture. By changing the lighting you can emphasize or suppress the background, and by choosing the appropriate lens you can include varying amounts of background. Again, you must consider the sort of portrait you want. A head and shoulders, or head only, shot may suffer from a distracting background in which case a standard or medium telephoto lens is probably the best choice. On the other hand, an 'environmental' picture, which includes the subject's surroundings, is suited to a moderate wide angle lens, with the subject sufficiently far away to avoid undue distortion. When using a wide angle, remember to photograph your subject more or less face on, to avoid distortion.

Portraits which include a good deal of background detail in this way are an interesting alternative to the more usual head and shoulders portrait. They provide space for many of those clues,

Boutique *A shop window provided the illumination for this striking study*
Couple at a window *Black and white film is better for a portrait in which the background is cluttered.*
Craftsman *Using natural light from the window, this photograph also includes tools to give a clue about the man and his work.*

black reflectors. The classic 'Rembrandt look', for example, uses strong side lighting, perhaps achieved with the help of black reflectors on one side to kill reflections and the careful use of white reflectors to give a little light in the shadows. This sort of lighting brings out character and bone structure, but it emphasizes facial features, making them more angular. Someone with a hard, bony face will not be flattered by such lighting, whereas flat lighting, with the subject facing a window, will help to soften their features. Similarly, a person with full features will look better with side lighting than with flat lighting.

The background to the portrait can

which, like the lines of experience, tell us a great deal about a person's character and life style. With older people in particular, the accumulation of personal trifles, pictures and souvenirs, are an essential part of that person. At the other end of the age scale, a child's first drawings and paintings form a natural background to a portrait. You could even engage a child's attention by asking him or her to draw or paint or draw something while you take the photographs.

As well as looking for these visual clues, the indoor photographer must also be on the lookout for potential distractions when deciding on the way to approach the shot.

A. J. Ayer *Harsh sidelighting with a reflector on the shadow side*
Chinese *Room lighting can often be quite adequate when using fast film*

Pay special attention to the wallpaper —a strong pattern is likely to be very noticeable, particularly in black and white.

If the background or lighting in one room are unsuitable, then try other rooms to achieve the best results. Also look at what the subject is wearing. Dark clothing in light surroundings is difficult to photograph, and rather than make life difficult for yourself the best solution might be to ask your subject to change.

Remember, however, that few people actually like being photographed, and for your subject the experience is perhaps less thrilling than it is for you. It is vital to be prepared before you start— assemble a good collection of reflectors and sheets, if you think you will need them, together with a range of clips, clamps, sticky tape and so on to help set them up without fuss.

Your choice of film depends on the circumstances. Fast films will be particularly useful, being both sensitive and comparatively low contrast. In black and white, you are mainly concerned with the strength and direction of the light, but when using colour slide material you must also consider the colour of the light.

As well as the problems of different colours of artificial light affecting your results, there are such unknown variables as the colour of the walls, and shifts of the colour of daylight when the sun goes behind a cloud. Given all these, the best solution may simply be to use fast colour negative film, so that colour corrections can be made during printing.

Whether you use fast or slow film, a tripod can be very helpful. As well as allowing you to use exposure times slower than 1/60 second, it enables you to keep the camera fixed while you vary the set up. It may be hard to achieve a relaxed, natural look, however, so the choice depends on you, your subject and the effect you want.

Old people

Whether you are taking a formal portrait or a candid shot, you will often find that elderly people make interesting and rewarding subjects. But the best results will be gained from the right approach

Photographing old people demands far more attention and consideration than many other types of work. While everyone has at some time snapped a candid shot of some elderly character, just as they might photograph any other interesting subject they happened to come across, anything more premeditated can call upon all a photographer's skills, both technical and social.

Why should anyone want to photograph an old person ? One reason might be that the person is a relative or friend who just happens to be elderly. But if the reason is that the old are photogenic, perhaps implying easy subjects who are unlikely to object to the invasion of their privacy, then be careful. It is all too easy to take pictures which are stereotyped and predictable, and which may even unintentionally insult the individual. It would be a simple matter to concentrate on the negative aspects of old age, and to miss the subtler insights into your subject's personality.

Many photographers feel that there is something intrinsically interesting about old people. The very fact of having 'made it' to some advanced age seems worth recording by the camera. This may be true, and in many cases could lead to a telling and interesting picture. But it is important to try to avoid the superficial, the easy and unkind photograph. The texture of the skin on an old person's face can result in an unusual picture, but we all know that the old look old, and in close-up older still.

If you think about the old people you know well, perhaps in your immediate family, you will realize that they have the same range of characteristics as younger people. Some are energetic, others aren't. Some are optimistic and humorous, others not. Some are gregarious, and so on. So be aware of the individual personality of your subject, and avoid the usual cliché which we so often associate with pictures of the old, namely the isolation of age.

Many people who reach advanced years have lost their partner in life. If this is the case with your chosen subject, consider including mementos of the past in your photograph. We accumulate so much ephemera in our passage through life that a picture which includes a favourite piece of furniture, or possession, can both create a visually interesting background and help to relax your subject. Such an approach allows you to make an implicit comment on loneliness, while at the same time placing the person firmly in a real and living world.

You may be asked to take a formal portrait of an elderly person in your family, a picture which will be placed in the family album. In the case of a widowed grandmother, for instance, you could place a framed portrait of the old lady's husband in your photograph

Conversation *The best candid shots are taken when the photographer is unseen—wait until your subjects are relaxed and preoccupied*

Double portrait *Standing well away from your subject and using a long lens to close in is less overwhelming, particularly to older people*

which may evoke feelings of sadness or memories of happy times in the past.

Remember that your subject's response will be dictated by the way you handle the photographic session. One way of creating the right atmosphere for a portrait of an elderly person, who may be quite nervous when confronted by a bewildering array of modern photographic equipment, is to encourage them to talk about the past. Here you might learn something which could help you achieve an unusual and interesting portrait.

If your model is a war veteran he may have medals, honours or awards which he only brings out once a year for a formal dinner. Or your subject may have a collection of stamps, matchboxes, teapots or butterflies. It really does not matter what it is, but to include the old person's past, or their special interest or skill, should produce a different, or at least an interesting photograph. After all, old people have had the experience that younger people admire. Most of them are very proud of this fact.

Home setting *Although the face is partly obscured, this indoor setting provides a wealth of information about the subject.*

When you ask about your subject's past life, or about the objects that surround him or her, your questions are bound to cause some nostalgia. It will be largely up to you whether you wish to depict sorrow or joy. Be gentle and considerate with your questions. Many old people are suspicious or secretive, and a sympathetic approach may result

in a favourite object being removed from a dark cupboard and brought into the daylight.

It is worth remembering that many old people, deprived of friends and relations through death or illness, will form special relationships with their pets. Unkind observers may well say that the pet, be it cat, dog, budgerigar or what-

lady holding her newly born grandchild. On the other hand look for the baffled expression of the old man in the street when he is confronted by a crowd of colourful youngsters.

The mood of your photograph will depend not just on the people or objects you choose to surround your subjects with, but also on the type of lighting you select. If you are considering a formal approach, remember that natural light, especially if diffused somewhat, is a kinder medium than artificial light. Think twice before using flash, for this can be very disconcerting for an elderly model who may be genuinely confused as to what is happening. Bear in mind that the best way to achieve a good portrait is to have a willing and relaxed subject. A photograph taken in natural light enables you to decide which is the right moment to press the shutter. Sometimes, if you have been chatting during the setting-up time, you might be able to shoot a few pictures surreptitiously.

Old and young *One way of emphasizing the qualities of old age is to contrast them with those of a much younger person in the same shot*

White cat *Photographing old people in their own homes, using available light rather than flash, can give a personal, intimate picture*

ever, is a child, husband or wife substitute. A more sympathetic view is that the animal is really a perfect friend for the elderly. It is loving and affectionate, dependant, and not too talkative! Portraits of old people with their pets can be extremely effective and very revealing of the person's character. We are all aware that just as people who live together for a long time can come to resemble one another, so human and pet can assume a curious affinity. Look carefully at old people with their animals—not just their expressions, but their stance or gait.

An old lady with her head cocked to one side may be talking to her canary who seems to be making the same gesture. A man in his best winter coat may be walking along with his dog who is also clad in a smart woollen coat. A woman peering out of a window, holding her cat, may be adopting the same expression of intense concentration as the animal. Such candid shots can occur at any time, so it is worth watching out for them with your camera ready.

The tenderness of old age towards youth, and the special communication that exists between widely differing generations can make for rewarding portraits of the old and young together. Double portraits of this kind make an immediate contact with the audience, and remind us of the inevitable progress from birth towards death. Look out for the striking difference in skin texture between the old and the young and emphasize this with careful lighting in your picture. Try to photograph the old

This is not possible if you have chosen to use flash.

Shooting pictures informally can produce excellent results. Again, be aware that there is always a likelihood when you are photographing strangers that people may become conscious of your presence. Say there is a family group, in the park or on a beach, where a lot of members of different ages are gathered together enjoying themselves. Imagine the shot you particularly want is of grandparents admiring or playing with their grandchildren. You only have a few seconds to get the picture before someone in the family becomes aware of your presence. Once this happens, show yourself to be friendly and that you are enjoying, from the viewpoint of an outsider, the activity of the family group. Smile, indicate the camera, shrug and shoot the picture. You have taken the shot and chances are nobody will be upset. The secret is to judge the mood of the moment, and respond to it. Such a family grouping will probably be delighted that their happiness is being shared by someone else. You might even be asked to shoot a few for their album!

A photograph of an old person outside and alone is a more delicate matter calling for tact and judgement. Here the secret is to avoid any sense of intrusion on their privacy, and should your presence be sensed and objected to, you must respect their wishes immediately. If you have a telephoto lens, you might be able to avoid any problem of this kind, but results will show you that standing back from your subject has built-in disadvantages. The flattening effect of long lenses does not always yield a con-

Look at me! *Photographs can often be more effective if the subject looks directly into the camera as with this violin maker.*

Laughter *Occasionally you may be rewarded with a subject who really enjoys being photographed and your shots can say much about the sitter*

vincing portrait, particularly in a situation you are not able to control. It is also difficult to place your subject in a recognizable background.

For example, an old person alone on a bench in the park taken with a long lens might allow you to make out details of expression, and include a portion of the seat. Behind, out of focus trees are all the lens will show. On a normal, or slightly wide angle lens, the shot shows that there is no-one else on the bench. A very wide angle lens can isolate that person on the bench, by showing quite clearly that there is no-one else around.

Ask yourself which of these you would choose as the more evocative and telling image. Each approach can tell a story or convey a mood, but in both cases the emphasis of the picture is quite different.

There is a danger of being over-cautious when lining up a subject. Some photographers lurk around with a lens

Back view *People have backs as well as fronts! Even without the subjects' faces this shot is very expressive and a nice comment on old age too*

Portrait *A more serious study often works better in black and white than colour, particularly if you want to convey the subject's character*

like a shotgun, stalking their quarry as if on a jungle expedition. Such behaviour, can often be as objectionable as a fish-eye lens jammed under the subject's nose. Bear in mind that most people do not object to their photographs being taken. (There are of course obvious exceptions. In some countries it is frowned upon, and photographs of the ill or injured may not endear you to those around.) Ask the subject's permission politely, and be prepared to stand up for your motives if questioned. You will find most old people flattered, if somewhat embarrassed, and mainly co-operative. In this respect they do not differ from anyone else. But do try leaving the telephoto in the camera bag, and go for the human touch. Your pictures will be all the better for it.

One area well worth exploring is that of traditional craftsmanship. Here the accent is very much on longevity, and many people work long past the usual retirement age once they have spent a long apprenticeship and a lifetime perfecting their skills. People who work with wood or glass, potters and painters, all make ideal photographic subjects. If you are able to convey a craftsman's skill, and something of the great concentration and attention the job requires, you are well on the way to achieving a worthwhile portrait.

For instance, Frederick Gandolfi, the only remaining maker of mahogany and brass plate cameras in England, and the last of his family line, poses regularly for his portrait. This is usually taken by a contented customer, with a Gandolfi camera!

Another gathering point for the elderly which will provide you with a rich and varied choice of weather-beaten, experienced, perceptive and humorous countenances is the local country fair. Wherever animals are put through their paces, you are bound to spot lines of elderly experts who have seen it all before. Country people are curious and competitive in these matters, and love looking over other people's pets, livestock and associated interests. These sorts of gatherings are particularly suitable for candid or intimate studies since your subject's concentration is directed elsewhere, and there is a great deal going on all around. Not just fairs, but gymkhanas, country races and markets offer plenty of rewards for the patient photographer.

Many elderly people are very active, and some sporting events organize special 'veteran' events. Tennis, golf and bowls appeal to a broad age group, and can be played well into old age. All activities where skill rather than physical strength is the main ingredient are worth keeping an eye on, such as darts, chess, card games and pool or billiards. You are sure to find a number of elderly, intense and concentrated faces, not only among the spectators but the competitors as well! Such situations allow you to set old people in a particular environment and show them at their best.

Portraits outdoors

Nearly everyone takes photographs of family and friends from time to time, but most photographers have a rather casual approach to the subject. A little thought and careful planning can improve your portraits dramatically

Taking someone's portrait is, perhaps, the most personal of all photographic assignments, and portraits are probably the most treasured of all photographs. Millions of wallets, walls, desks and mantlepieces the world over are adorned with pictures of faces which are loved and cherished.

But the magic of creating a photo that instantly captures the look and personality of a friend or relative has very little to do with cameras and equipment. Successful portraiture—recording and preserving the likeness of someone—depends as much on the photographer seeing and shooting at the right time and in the right place.

The best advice for any photographer wanting to succeed in revealing a flattering yet recognizable likeness of a friend or relative on film is to think about your subject before the session.

Bronzed *Strong sunlight brings out the rich gold of the suntanned skin but the face is kept in shadow to avoid harsh and unflattering modelling*

Looking in *The child's face glows against the dark window surround and warmly wrapped coat and peeps appealingly into the corner of the frame*

What are the pleasing or outstanding characteristics about him or her, and how could you successfully translate them onto film?

The best place to start taking portraits is outdoors. The light is far brighter than indoors, offering a wide choice of possibilities ranging from the strong harsh sunlight on the beach to the deep shadow of the woodland floor on a rainy day. The number of potential settings is also enormous—gardens, shopping arcades, mountains, fields and so on. And taking portraits outdoors can often be spontaneous. You might decide to take a friend's portrait on the spur of the moment, while walking across the park, for instance.

Spontaneity can be vital because in a formal situation people tend to become self-conscious and expressions become forced. Most people are terribly anxious and shy about having their photograph taken, and may be apprehensive about the finished result.

Until your subject is relaxed, it can be difficult to get a good portrait. The art is to make the session an enjoyable event for both subject and photographer. If it all feels like a chore, that is how the results will look. Be prepared to use a lot of film on the session, letting the subject get used to the camera and waiting for the right expression.

Talk to your subject. Tell jokes. If you want a relaxed atmosphere, you have to be at ease yourself. Confidence and a friendly manner are an essential part of achieving good portraits. You will probably need practice before you can relax and take control because, unlike your subject, you will be doing two things at once—talking and trying to take the shot.

Portraiture essentially involves two people, the photographer and subject, and it is normally expected that the

Old man *A man portrayed against a background of the work that occupies over half his life. The rough texture of the skin encouraged a close up*

photographer should take the initiative. Unless your subject is a professional model or actor, it is not enough to simply place him or her in front of the camera and press the shutter. You have to direct your subject in the nicest and friendliest possible way.

Overdirecting, however, can be worse than not directing at all. If you force your subject into a pose, he will resent it and feel like a helpless puppet and ill-at-ease. It will also almost certainly produce a 'stuffed portrait'. On the other hand, it is not enough to just say 'smile' and hope for the best.

The happy medium, wherever possible, is to make your subject feel that he or she is a valuable part of the creative process. Get him to take a positive part in the session and suggest new poses. These may be more natural to him. He may feel awkward standing up, for instance, and lean against a wall or sit down to make himself comfortable. Unless you have positive reasons for the upright pose, you should encourage changes of position.

Many people become very self-conscious about their hands when sitting for a portrait and you should always suggest to your subject what to do with them. You might, for instance, want a casual impression and might suggest that his hands go in his pockets. Or you could give him something to hold.

But remember that hands can contribute to the composition. Hands are a very important means of expression and may draw attention to some feature of character that would be missed, or hard

Man and his dog *Animals can say a lot about personality. The mutual respect and affection clear in this picture suggest a gentle but strong willed man*

ever, in which case you want to find the angle that obscures the less attractive or weaker parts of the face. A broad face, particularly a broad chin, can be made to look narrower by shooting from a high angle and getting the subject to tilt his or her chin away from the camera. A weak chin, on the other hand, can be made to look stronger by shooting slightly upwards from a low angle.

As well as thinking carefully about your subject you will need to consider the setting. Ideally, the background should relate in some way to your subject. What should be avoided are backgrounds which dominate by being too strong or intricate. The idea is that the setting should complement and enhance the subject.

Mood can be accentuated with lighting and outdoors there are many ways light can be used creatively.

The best all-round illumination for photographing people is evenly diffused light—soft, flattering shadows can be produced with the filtered, hazy light of a misty morning or in a shaded setting, such as in a wood or under a tree. Bright cloudy days are particularly good. In addition, subjects often feel more comfortable in this sort of lighting than they do in direct sunlight, which can make them squint.

However, soft light may sometimes hide the very character lines you wish to bring out. Unless you want to hide their wrinkles, weather-beaten faces need strong direct light to bring out the rich skin texture.

The point to remember is that you are responsible for whatever is in the frame of your camera. Look at it carefully, and especially train yourself to be aware of distractions, such as a lamp post coming

Johnny Morris *Hands can be a problem in portraits, but they were kept nicely occupied for this picture to provide a relaxed and informal portrait*

to show, in a simply facial portrait. A thoughtful person, for instance, might rest his chin on his hand. An ebullient person may place his hands definitely on his knees when sitting or on his waist when standing. Cupped or open hands can sometimes suggest vulnerability. However the hands are used, though, they should look part of your subject's natural repertoire of hand movements.

Thinking about your subject and looking for his or her best attributes will help you to decide how to take the photo. If he or she has attractive eyes, for instance, close in on the face. The wrinkled faces of some older people may be so fascinating that a close-up of the face alone provides a strong and interesting image.

Many photographers are unsure how to approach close-ups. Should the subject look at the camera obliquely or stare straight into the camera? Or should he not look at the camera at all?

Most people nowadays tend to prefer an oblique shot, often with the head

slightly tilted, because this seems more natural and unforced. A head-on approach, on the other hand, although it often seems horribly formal, can produce striking portraits of forceful characters. Shots like this can be very direct, and even intimidating, to the viewer. Whatever approach you choose, however, it should be appropriate to the person you are trying to portray.

If you move round to shoot from an angle, beware of going too far. Too sharp an angle can lose you all the detail and information on one side of the face. Because of this, profiles rarely work for portraits, though they can make fascinating abstracts. A profile shot is generally only successful when the subject has very distinctive features.

Your aim might be to take a photo that particularly flatters your subject, how-

Artur Rubinstein *This charming portrait of a famous musician shows that a successful picture does not need an obvious musical background*

44

Full-length or close-up ? *Three different crops of the same photograph show how the format can considerably alter the impression conveyed by the picture. All three versions are strong shots, but all say something entirely different about the personality of the* *subject. The close-up is a striking portrait of an attractive woman. The shot below shows her as a mother with her child. But it needs the three-quarter length shot to show her as she really is and how she lives, through the clues of her stance and her surroundings*

out of your subject's head or a strand of hair that has cast an ugly shadow.

Although good portraits can be taken on virtually any equipment, there is something to be said for choosing a lens to suit the type of shot you have in mind. For head-and-shoulders shots, an 85-120 mm zoom, or a fixed focal length telephoto within the same range, are probably best because you have to stand farther back than you would with the standard lens. This reduces the chances of distortion of features close to the camera—close-ups with a standard lens can often produce huge noses or overprominent chins. Another advantage with long lenses for close-up work is that you subdue sharp, overdistinct features flatteringly. Remember, though, that this could work against you if the subject has very shallow features. One

Girl in a straw Hat *Diffuse lighting is ideal for romantic portraits of young girls. Here the straw hat both softens the light and frames the face*

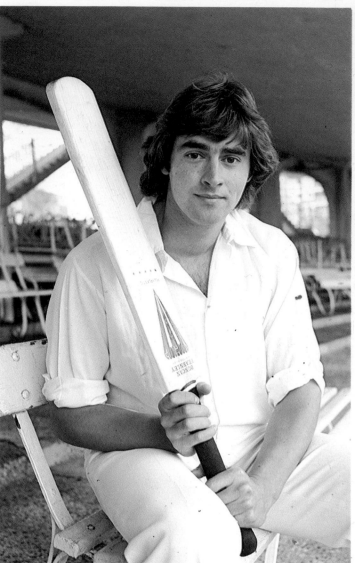

Unusual viewpoint *Changing the angle of your shots can produce dramatic changes in mood. These can be particularly effective in black and white; this shot might well look weak in colour*

Cricketer *One of the best ways to portray people is to catch them at their favourite activity or in their working environment. Here a cricketer's bat is a useful prop and a sign of his trade*

final point in favour of a short telephoto is that the comparatively narrow depth of field allows you to keep the background blurred more easily.

With half- or full-length shots, however, it is probably better to retain your standard lens. You may even wish to use a wide angle lens for these shots for special effects. A short person can look very tall if photographed from a low angle with a wide angle lens. And even with close-ups you may be able to use a short focal length lens to create a dynamic and moody impression, but with this sort of shot you must choose your viewpoint carefully or the result could be bizarre.

But whatever equipment you use, the success of your portraits depends ultimately upon your relationship with your subject and the confidence that comes from experience and a keen interest in the people that you portray.

Happy couple *Shots like this depend less on careful posing than establishing a rapport with your subject. It is virtually impossible to fake laughter*

Hair colouring *The success of such a portrait depends entirely on capturing the arresting hair style and dress and minimizing background distractions*

Candid photography

People can be the most fascinating subjects of all. But taking candid photographs requires diplomacy and understanding as well as a practised eye if you want to capture life as it happens.

Posed deliberately in front of the camera, nearly everyone becomes a little self-conscious. For this reason, many people feel that the only way to get natural and totally candid portraits is to catch people by surprise or, better still, without them knowing at all.

By exploiting the ability of the modern camera to freeze an instant, men and women can be pictured going about their lives in their normal environment, and fleeting expressions or moments of human drama can be transformed into striking permanent images. Taking pictures of people without their knowledge may seem a little unfair, but it certainly produces some fascinating results.

The word 'candid' means, literally, 'frankly truthful'. Related to photography, however, it has come to mean 'unposed', and candid photography can be approached in one of two ways. You can either go out deliberately to provoke a reaction and attract your subject's attention. Or you can try to avoid being noticed at all and try to capture life as it happens.

The fascination of the first approach is capturing people's snap response to the camera, whether it be surprise, hostility or laughter. It is an ideal way of taking informal portraits of friends and family, and many shots of this type are taken by framing up the subject unobtrusively, attracting their attention and then shooting. But it can also produce dramatic results in less familiar situations.

Surprise photographs of strangers, for example, can produce a whole variety of interesting responses. Strangers will react to the camera in different ways. Some will enjoy the attention and play up to the camera. Others may be resentful and sullen or even aggressive. Some may simply be surprised. Whatever the response, though, the results can be very revealing.

Reaction shots

Because most people react positively to the camera—if only to positively ignore it—press photographers and photojournalists often use this technique to portray people in their own environment. If, for instance, they want to illustrate life in a really depressed urban area, this sort of reaction shot often gives the impact that the photographer wants. It might be that the surprised or aggressive look on the subject's face is simply a response to the suddenness of the camera's intrusion, but the result conveys the tough environment far more strongly than any posed photo would.

In its extreme form, this sort of photojournalism becomes posed rather than candid and many colour supplement pictures are taken by placing the subject deliberately in his or her natural environment. A shepherd, therefore, would be photographed against a back-

Girl in a window *Washing-lines across the subject are usually distracting, but here they add to the natural look and to the moodiness of the picture*

ground of sheep and green hills, a docker against ships and cranes and an architect against his own buildings.

The kind of response depends to a considerable extent on the photographer. An aggressive, impatient photographer will generally get a similar response and may be lucky if the hostility is only recorded on film. Unless that is the sort of photo you want, then you should behave with consideration towards your subject and remember that you are indeed intruding.

Whatever the response, though, these reaction shots are, to many photographers, rarely candid—truly candid shots are only taken when the subject is

totally unaware that there is someone around with a camera. People are pictured doing normal things—sleeping, waiting for a bus, talking in the streets, buying the groceries—in their natural environment. The idea is to show people as they really are or to capture a fleeting moment of humour or pathos, anger or kindness. The camera must be a detached and totally unnoticed observer. The photographer's job is never to arrange the subject; but simply to spot the situation 'frame up' and decide on the moment to capture the situation with the maximum impact.

Shooting unobserved

This sort of picture can be taken anywhere—the only essential ingredient is people. As long as there are people around, there is potential for a candid shot. Crowded places naturally provide plenty of scope, but an isolated figure can often provide a poignant subject. But it is important that the photographer remains largely unobserved, and it helps if people are absorbed in their own activities rather than ready to look round at the first click.

Taking candid pictures unobserved on a crowded rush hour station, for instance, is generally fairly easy because everyone is concentrating on getting home. Unfortunately it can be difficult spotting potential subjects and getting them in focus in the fast moving crowd.

On a crowded beach, on the other hand, there is much less movement, but people are less absorbed in what they are doing. Not surprisingly, many candid beach pictures just show people asleep

A bird on the head *Children make ideal subjects for candid work, so when out with children keep your camera prepared for amusing moments*

Lady *Candid photographs can be direct and revealing portraits, but shots like this require an eye for an arresting face, a gentle approach and a sure technique*

in deck chairs or reading newspapers. Places where movement is slow or predicatable but where everyone is sufficiently absorbed to leave the photographer unobserved make the best locations for candid photography. Markets have plenty of potential. So too have crowds at outdoor events.

Candid pictures often tend to be of older people or are set in working class urban districts. This is not necessarily because such subjects are more photogenic, but often because they are easier to photograph. In areas of densely populated terraced housing, there are usually plenty of people walking around; in affluent and spacious suburbs, the few people around tend to be in cars. Old people are similarly easier to photograph because they are generally slower moving and have more time to stop and pass the time of day with friends in the street. And while young people tend to be much the same the world over, older people often retain local dress and traditions.

Again, while candid shots are to be found anywhere at any time, there are occasions when it is easier to shoot unobtrusively. In summer, plenty of people are on the streets and there are many potential subjects. In winter, on the other hand, there are fewer people around, but you tend to be less obtrusive, particularly if you wear a heavy coat to conceal your camera. It is possible to stand shooting for hours on a street corner on a gloomy winter's day without anyone noticing, but you will be spotted instantly in your shirt sleeves in the summer sunshine.

Washing the pony *People absorbed in some task are again ideal for candid shots and you often have time to compose your picture leisurely and properly*

help you become accustomed to the idea of taking impromptu shots of people before you try your technique on total strangers.

It is often thought that the best way to take candid pictures without being noticed is to use all sorts of elaborate equipment—concealed cameras, subminiatures, telephotos—but these are usually unnecessary. Indeed, people are understandably suspicious and resentful of these 'sneaky' techniques and in some countries the surreptitious use of a miniature camera can be positively dangerous. Some people suggest that a twin-lens reflex camera, of the sort traditionally used by wedding photographers, held at waist level is the ideal for candid work because it is much less obvious when you shoot. But you can generally take pictures much faster with an SLR, and an eye-level viewpoint is generally more pleasing, although it may be worth bending down or shooting from above to create a bit of variety.

There is one drawback to using an SLR, however, and that is its noisiness. While it is very useful to be able to focus quickly and accurately, the system that allows you to do this, with a mirror that must flip out of the way before the

But wherever and whenever you go out to take candid pictures, it is important to attract the minimum attention. Bright, flashy clothes are clearly out, but so too is a flashy, aggressive manner. The best candid shots are taken not by a cartoon-image loud, khaki-clad press photographer bristling with lenses and equipment, but by the quiet observer.

If you cannot help being noticed when you arrive at your location, wait for a while and let people get used to you and your camera before you start shooting in earnest. Unfortunately, you will rarely remain unobserved for long and even if your subject does not react, other people, may interrupt your activities. If this happens, you must be patient and polite—any sort of argument will ruin the situation—and carry on shooting if possible.

Many photographers avoid candid photography because they find it embarassing, particularly if they are noticed. There are no easy answers to this problem and it is up to the individual photographer to overcome it. However, many of the most experienced candid photographers suffered from self-consciousness when they started and gaining confidence is largely a matter of practice. Nevertheless, it may be worth going along to the local amateur dramatic society to take pictures during rehearsals. Obviously you must get permission first, but most actors and actresses will be only too pleased to have their performances on film. This should

Crowd shots *Spectators at a sports event make good subjects—they are usually too absorbed to notice cameras. Try to concentrate on a few faces*

Café *A viewpoint need not necessarily be an extreme—here crouching helped the overall composition and avoided attracting the subject's attention*

On the beach *With people at play and plenty of light, crowded holiday beaches provide plenty of scope for catching revealing moments on film*

picture can be taken, gives a noticeable click as you press the shutter.

Some SLRs are less noisy than others, but quietest of all are non-SLRs which do not have mirrors or focal plane shutters. This is where compact cameras come into their own, since they generally have comparatively silent leaf shutters. Twin-lens reflex cameras, of the sort mentioned above, also have leaf shutters and offer the additional advantages of accurate focusing and interchangeable lenses.

Speed is perhaps the most important factor in candid photography—not so much the shutter speed or the speed of the film, but the speed with which you can decide on the framing, focusing and exposure, and take the shot. Any time lost here may lose you the picture or may give your subject time to see you. Automatic exposure and focusing certainly help in this respect, but neither of these will make much difference if you are not alert or, more significantly, unfamiliar, with your equipment. It is essential to be completely at home with your camera if you are to operate quickly and unobtrusively. Seconds spent fumbling with the focusing and

aperture can only help draw attention and may prove embarrassing. The famous candid photographer, Henri Cartier-Bresson, once claimed to be able to adjust the focus, aperture and shutter speed while the camera was still in his pocket!

In fact, it is rarely necessary to readjust all the settings for each individual shot. When you go out for a day of candid photography in a particular location, the same settings will probably be adequate for most of the day, unless you go into dark shadows or shoot from extremely close quarters. On a bright, cloudy day outdoors, for instance, a setting of *f*/8 at 1/125 of a second will give the correct exposure in most candid situations. It will also give you reasonable depth of field and you can be sure that if you set the focus to around 3 metres, or whatever the average shooting distance is, your picture will probably be sharp.

Candid lenses

There is something to be said for all focal lengths and lens types. A telephoto will allow you to fill the frame without getting too close and may get you pictures of inaccessible subjects, but the result will look as distant and detached as indeed you are. Pictures taken with a standard or wide angle lens are far more immediate and involved, but have to be

taken at a much closer range. Nevertheless, you may be able to photograph someone with a wide angle lens even if he sees the camera if you only include him or her at the edge of the frame—people rarely believe they are being photographed unless the camera is pointing straight at them. Furthermore, such a lens will include some background—often invaluable to help place subjects in their normal environments. Most professionals are happiest with a standard lens, or a 28-50 mm zoom, and only use a long lens when absolutely necessary.

However you tackle candid photography, you must remember that not everyone appreciates having their picture taken, particularly if the result could be embarrassing. Indeed, it is well known that some people, such as the African Masai tribe, find it highly worrying. The Masai believe that if you take their picture you take away their souls—though they may accept financial compensation. Either way, you must consider the feelings of the people you photograph. It might be a nice gesture to offer them a copy of your final shot.

Touch of class *You need a quick eye to take advantage of situations like the above. The shot is even more amusing since the occasion is so formal and that this gesture quite furtive.*

Gone fishing *Fay Godwin took advantage of the early evening light to get this candid family silhouette. The small boy looking up to his father establishes a point of interest.*

Motorbike yoga *From time to time, when they think no-one is looking, some people revert to strange practices. This man seems to have turned himself into a yogi. Or it could be that he just fell off his bike! On the other hand it could be a set-up photo.*

Poodle and chauffeur *This intriguing picture seems to be a lucky candid shot caught in passing. In fact, the car was spotted on a day when the photographer, Thurston Hopkins, was without his camera. He pursued the unusual pair in a taxi and discovered that the man owned a car hire firm and took the poodle for a ride whenever he had some spare time. He was happy to pose the next day. Humorous moments are not usually re-created with much success, but this shot is an exception.*

Pause for thought *Photographs like this are effective because they capture mood when the subject is unselfconscious, like this young musician who is obviously exhausted after a long and gruelling rehearsal. A photograph like this is well worth waiting for.*

Chapter 3
People in action
On the beach

All too often, photographs taken on a beach end up as a disappointment—large, empty stretches of plain sand and few areas of interest to break up the monotony. The beach itself rarely works as a subject on its own—but it is certainly an ideal general background, and the photographer must look for additional subjects to add interest.

Photography on a sunny beach, however, also involves more practical problems—extremely high light levels, loose sand blowing around and the hazard of being close to salt water. Professional photographer John Garrett decided that his ideal holiday camera would be a Nikonos IV-A—a rugged all weather viewfinder camera with aperture priority automatic exposure control. It also has the unusual capacity of being at home underwater or covered with sand.

John decided that it would be more interesting to concentrate on people enjoying themselves in and around the water—children, sunbathers, candids. And, with the Nikonos, he had the added advantage of being able to take photographs underwater. Using the marine capability of the camera, John tried photographing one of his sons in the swimming pool, but for a more unusual image he held the camera so the lens was only half in the water. He also found that the camera was very useful for taking pictures of people splashing about in the waves.

Since the refraction of water makes images appear larger, the Nikonos camera is usually fitted with one of the wide angle lenses that are available. Even though an 80 mm lens is made for the Nikonos, John was happy to be able to use his conventional SLR with a telephoto lens for candid shots and other close-up work. Since the slowest timed speed of the Nikonos is 1/30 second, John also found that he needed an ordinary camera for low light work—such as the shot of the yacht framed through the palm trees.

To cope with the bright light levels, John used slow transparency film. The only problem with this is that it has limits when it comes to dealing with wide ranges of contrast. For this reason John tried to avoid shots including both extremes of brightness, such as sand,

Gulls *John chose a small aperture, so the camera selected a slow shutter speed to emphasize the birds' movement*

54

and extremes of shade, such as that under a parasol. Most of his subjects were fairly evenly lit and in this way he was able to make the most of the bright colours which slow films offer.

Photographer Nigel Snowdon approaches the problems in a different way for surf action down under.

If a photographer can manage to keep valuable equipment away from the sand and spray, a surf carnival offers plenty to photograph. Although such an event is slightly different from most of Nigel's I found the 16 mm was particularly good for this—it gets everything in the frame but also produces an interesting effect. My 180 mm lens was also useful for picking out characteristic details and isolating them from the background.

However, since the most exciting action takes place in the surf, Nigel decided that a long focus lens was essential. His bitingly sharp 400 mm ED Nikkor was ideal for this—sometimes even used with a Nikon X2 converter. The bright midday sun allowed him to use Kodachrome 64 with a shutter speed of 1/500 second and still be able to stop down to around f/8 or f/11. The fast shutter speed froze the spray in mid air and prevented any camera shake with the longer lenses. Even so, Nigel had to use as monopod to help support the 400 mm telephoto, especially when the shutter was pressed.

Ready to plunge
A blue graduated filter on a 20 mm lens darkened the sky. **On the waves** *Without a long telephoto—here a 400 mm—subjects would be too small*

Relaxing in the sun
John looked for contrasting colours that would add interest to his shots—here, splashes of gold, yellow and blue
In the sea *Making the camera choose a fast speed by using a wide aperture, John found the Nikonos came into its own in the surf. The fast shutter speed caught the child and the water in mid air to make a good action shot* **In the pool** *The Nikonos can also be partially submerged to provide an unusual image* **Eye shades** *John found a conventional camera and a telephoto lens more useful for candid shots*

Weddings

Wedding photographs are frequently dull and formal and give only a hint of the full flavour of the event— but with a little thought and careful planning, you should be able to take a series of attractive shots

If you look at any family wedding album, you will see that the style of traditional wedding photography has changed very little over the years. Most couples, when planning a formal wedding, will hire a professional photographer to take pictures for an album that they will keep for the rest of their lives, and probably pass on to their children after them.

The official photographer has a difficult role to play—he must direct and organize people who may be nervous and preoccupied with such an important day, and probably not at their most co-operative, and he does not have a second chance to put things right if they turn out badly. So if the couple happen to ask you, as a friend, to take their official photographs, think twice before you accept. Mistakes on your part could ruin both the couple's day and your own— and at worst, you could lose your friends. Also remember that should your equipment fail, maybe without your knowledge, the blame will be on your shoulders and the couple will have no photographs at all. It is best to advise the couple to use an expert for the official coverage of the occasion, which will relieve you of a considerable responsibility and will not rob a professional of his livelihood. It will also allow you to concentrate on the more informal and creative photographs—aspects which are rarely in a professional's brief.

As quite often happens in such cases your friends may well find your informal pictures more natural and more interesting than the official version, and yours may be the photograph that is chosen to be framed for the mantlepiece, while the professional's pictures remain buried in a dusty album.

Whether you are taking your own informal pictures or have agreed to be the 'official' photographer, as a friend you have the tremendous advantage over a professional of knowing the couple concerned, and perhaps many of the family and friends. The aspect of personality is one that you could choose to bring out in your photographs, for a wedding provides a marvellous opportunity to take pictures of people, whether they are candid shots of the guests enjoying themselves, formal pictures of the ceremony itself, or portraits of the bride, groom and family.

One of the first opportunities for an informal portrait, if you are a friend of the family, occurs at the bride's home before the ceremony. Most brides will be nervous before such an occasion, so try to be reassuring and try not to use flash. If you keep your equipment to a minimum, perhaps using a fast film and a medium length telephoto lens, you will be able to stand back a little while the proud mother puts the finishing touches to her daughter's dress or make up, or the bridemaids rearrange the flowers. In this way you can take some informal shots of the preparations without upsetting anyone or getting in the way.

If you do not know the bride's family well, and cannot ask to visit their home first, try to reach the church or registry office early, so that you can photograph the bridegroom and other people of interest arriving at the scene. If you are early, you will have the chance to assess the lighting conditions, and to decide on the best position for you to adopt once the ceremony has begun. Remember that it may be distracting and impolite to wander around during the service, so choose your position with care. You should ask the vicar, priest or other authority for permission to take photographs. Most people will not mind a discreet picture taken without flash during a service, but photography is not usually allowed in synagogues.

The professional will be expected to cover the signing of the register and will take some flash pictures of the couple walking down the aisle. It may be difficult in these situations to find the room to achieve your own pictures, so it may be an idea to position yourself outside the church ready to take your photos, while the professional is busy lining up groups for the official pictures.

Group photographs are the most difficult part of wedding photography, particularly if you have taken on the task of official photographer, and they can be a real test of a photographer's skill and imagination. Traditionally, there should be a picture of the bride and groom with the bridesmaids, pages and best man, followed by a picture of the same group with the couple's parents. Finally a picture of this group with all the relations is usually taken.

The bigger the group, the more shots are needed to ensure that nobody is making a face or looking away at the crucial moment. If you are taking the official photographs, it is your job to arrange the group attractively and decisively, without keeping people hanging around for too long. If you do keep people waiting, the results will show up clearly in your pictures as a group of very bored and impatient people. It is a good idea to think about the group shots beforehand—visit the location in advance to find out how much space you will have, and what sort of a background you may have to use, bearing in mind that car parks and streets may be full of cars on the day.

Reception *An excellent time for candid shots—if you position yourself behind the couple, you can catch the expressions of people talking to them*

Whatever the group consists of, try to avoid the conventional line-up. A line of more than four or five people looks monotonous, and it is an idea to break the group up into rows, if you can possibly do so. Church steps are often used by official photographers for this reason because they help to break up the wedding group into staggered lines, without the danger of one person's face being hidden by another. Sloping ground may help to give you the same effect, but if the location has neither, an arrangement of two lines with the faces of the taller members in the back row showing between those in front works very well. The composition can look more interesting if the ends of the rows are curved in slightly towards the camera, or if the camera is positioned higher than usual.

Whatever the group arrangement, remember that a tripod will be essential, since you will need to move between camera and group to make adjustments. Close attention to detail is crucial.

Arrival *To take some informal photographs as the bride arrives, choose a spot carefully beforehand. Time will be limited and rushing around will only increase the tension*

Anticipation *On the other hand, be prepared to act quickly and take advantage of candid shots while some guests are distracted*

Signing the register *Many such shots are spoiled by cluttered backgrounds and fixed smiles—move in close to fill the frame and try to provoke an amusing and natural expression*

Look at the time! *This picture has all the elements of a good candid shot—you could quite easily set up something similar to give some of your photos a lighthearted touch*

Make sure that every shot is well focused, with ample depth of field. Give longer exposure times than normal, if necessary, in order to get good depth of field. Scan the scene carefully for waste paper and background objects such as cars. And if the churchyard or street outside the registry office is entirely unsuitable as a location, you can always assemble the groups later on at the reception, where the scenery may be more pleasant. If you decide that you want a really informal group, it will be much better to take the photographs at the reception, where everybody will be more relaxed.

If the professional photographer is the one responsible for the group shots, it may be interesting, and perhaps informative, to see how he handles them. Some professionals tend to overdirect people taking endless shots to ensure that everybody in the group is looking their best. Others manage to achieve excellent results in a very few minutes by their cheerful yet authoritative manner which is the hallmark of a good photographer.

Although, in this case, you will not be able to arrange your own groups, this is a marvellous opportunity to take candid shots of the group, or even of individual members of the group. It is best to stand back, to one side of the professional, using a telephoto lens to take these shots. While the formal groups are being directed, you have a great chance between the official pictures when people take a brief opportunity to relax. Quite often one of the group makes a joke or a comment at which everybody laughs. These are the moments which will provide you with a much more lively record of the occasion, so do not miss them! After all, if everything goes wrong—the wind blows, the bride's veil takes off, the bridesmaids burst into tears and the page keeps running out of the group to mummy, the professional will be the one who tears his hair out because he cannot achieve a single successful photograph, but you will have a splendid set of original candid shots, which everybody will enjoy after the event.

One of the most important pictures of the day is the portrait of the bride and groom together after the ceremony. It is worth finding a quiet spot in a more natural setting, rather than the formal background of the church door, where everybody is probably staring at you and the couple as well. Here again, it may be better to shoot the portrait later on at the reception, when they will be more relaxed, and their feelings of happiness and love for each other may not be so buried underneath a nervous exterior. If they do not respond well when staring at the camera, ask them to talk quietly to each other, or at least look at each other while you are photographing them. Take a mixture of head and shoulders shots and full-length pictures, if you can. Many couples want romantic, soft focus photographs of themselves, and if you are the official photographer it may be a good idea to ask them what sort of photograph they would really like. They may come up with some interesting ideas for you. If the reception is held at the birde's home, or even at a hotel, try to find a quiet room or a location outside where you can photograph them without the distractions of other people. Soft light falling through a window can produce a more natural effect than flash, and a home setting may be more attractive than a church door.

The reception itself usually begins with the bride and groom and their parents introducing themselves to all the guests. This is certainly worth photographing discreetly from a distance, with a medium length telephoto lens so as not to disturb the proceedings. Once the guests have been introduced and settle into the food and drink, they begin to relax and enjoy themselves. This is an excellent time for candid photography, since they will certainly not want to be organized into groups for formal photographs again. If you have a fairly quick eye, you can catch some amusing and delightful moments at the reception as people of different generations, old friends, relations, and even the not so friendly come together with an interest in common. The tension of the occasion begins to wear off completely at this stage, and people who have up to now been restricted by their formal attire, become happy, talkative, and even uninhibited.

This is not only the best time for candid photography, but it is probably the best time to ask the bride to pose for a few special pictures, whether or not you are the official photographer. Ideally, you will have already chosen your location and thought about the type of portrait you want. If so, you can approach her with confidence, and not waste too much of her time.

A portrait of the bride alone calls for some tact. Clearly, she will want to look her best, and you must decide which are her good features and try to give these prominence in your picture. If she has

beautiful hair or eyes, for instance, make sure that your composition and your choice of lighting make the most of such important features (see pages 32 to 36). On the other hand, she may have an unattractive quality which your photographs could help to obscure. If she is generously proportioned, ask her to stand at an angle to the camera or use

side lighting, which will be more flattering to her figure. Alternatively, concentrate on a head and shoulders shot. If necessary, use soft focus to hide any facial blemishes or poor make-up.

Backlighting can be particularly effective with this type of portrait, and will give you a much softer, more romantic image. Remember that the bride will

Look at that!
The best candid shots are taken while people are preoccupied

Formal group
For small group shots, look for a pleasant background

Informal group
Everyone relaxes after the service— look for people laughing

In the coach
Shooting through the coach from the far side as the couple leave can give a nicely framed shot

Bride at home
Using a long lens to remain unobtrusive, you can find good, unposed shots as the bride prepares

have gone to a lot of trouble to choose her dress, and will want to show it off to its best advantage in these pictures. Take care that the dress is arranged well, and that your lighting is kind to the texture of the material, particularly if it is made of silk or lace. If she is wearing a veil, make sure that it is not at an awkward angle, and does not run the risk of blowing over her face just as you fire the shutter. As with the portrait of both bride and groom together, you will find that natural lighting, with a fill-in reflector or flash if necessary, will give you better results.

At some stage during the reception there will be speechmaking, which is another marvellous opportunity for candid photography. Do not take pictures of a nervous speaker, or you may cause further embarrassment. Wait until the speech is over, when the subject is relieved that the ordeal is over, and is probably smiling. However, if you are lucky enough to be presented with a humorous or articulate speechmaker, you may well find that this person will respond, and even be encouraged by, your photography.

After the father of the bride has made his speech, the best man follows, reading the telegrams and introducing the bridegroom, who concludes these formalities. Keep a look out for the reactions of the couple, or even an elderly relative, to the traditionally suggestive remarks made by the best man in his speech.

If you are taking the official pictures, you will be expected to include the cutting of the cake, which usually follows these speeches. Remember that you can direct the action, if necessary, and may ask for the knife to be repositioned after the first cut so that you achieve a good shot. You may have to use flash for this picture, but bear in mind that direct flash may flatten details, especially on the white dress and cake, so try to use bounced flash if you are happy with your ability to do this and the room is not too large.

The moment when the bride disappears to change into her going-away outfit is not the cue for you to relax as photographer. Traditionally this is the moment when the best man and friends play their games of decorating the couple's car in some ridiculous and embarrassing fashion.

Finally, the bride and groom emerge to say their farewells and depart for their honeymoon. You will now have a last chance to photograph their exit, and the cheering crowds that follow them.

A wedding is one occasion at which the amateur photographer has a chance of taking pictures that will be really appreciated. It is also one occasion at which it is much better to use colour negative film rather than transparencies. People can look at prints much more easily when selecting them, and they will prefer to have a print to frame, or put into an album. It is worth asking a professional lab to make enlarged contact sheets, which are easier to view than the smaller contacts. Be sure to take ample supplies of film: a professional may use something like 30 rolls of film, while many amateurs will take no more than five. But it is better to have too much film than to run out at the wrong moment.

However creative you want to be with your wedding photography, remember that the people who choose a traditional wedding are most likely to be those who want the more traditional and conservative type of photograph. If you are aiming to sell your pictures, it may not pay you to be too unconventional in your approach. Use your skill and judgement to make your photographs more than just a plain record of the days' events.

The church *From the back of the church you can photograph the service and the interior without disturbing anyone*

Head and shoulders *Close-ups are rare, but can be effective, particularly if the bride has an attractive head-dress*

Outdoor sporting events

Photographing sport can be hard work—you can sit for hours for one shot—but once you develop an eye for action the rewards amply justify the effort

Few subjects provide a greater range of photogenic material than sport. Action and drama, atmosphere and colour—sport has it all. Whatever type of picture you want to take, a sporting event seems to offer a wealth of possibilities.

Action is there in abundance—the athlete sprinting for the ribbon, the burly forward powering his way out of a ruck—but there are many other photographic opportunities. If you want pictures of human drama, for instance, what better place to look than on the sports field?

If you are simply looking for attractive pictures, there is endless potential in the grace of the gymnast or the sparkle and colour of windsurfing. And when there is little happening on the field of play there are usually plenty of fascinating shots to be found in the crowd.

So where do you go to take good sports photos? Good pictures can be taken anywhere, at any sporting event, and it requires the skill of the photographer to seek them out. Nevertheless, some sports are much easier to photograph than others.

Looking for action

Any sport where there is plenty of natural action makes an excellent starting point for the budding sports photographer. Rugby's heaving scrums, crushing tackles and flying touch-downs provide plenty of scope for action shots. Tennis and football provide similarly good opportunities. And if you are able to get there, you can hardly go wrong with an Alpine skiing event for subject matter, with its high speed twists and turns, dramatic take-offs and spectacular falls. Although the vast expanse of snow presents a number of technical problems with exposure, these are easily overcome by careful positioning and judicious use of a light meter. Basically, though, any sport with plenty of large scale moments makes a good subject.

Where action is slow or small scale, however, exciting pictures can be difficult to find. Cricket might seem to be the obvious example, and certainly it is not an easy sport to cover, but there are many shots to be had in the bowler's run-up and delivery, and, because much of the action takes place in the same position every time, the camera can always be ready to fire at the right moment. While cricket may be slow moving for television, the photographer with the still camera can isolate the sporadic moment of high drama to create surprisingly lively pictures.

Getting exciting pictures from golf or swimming, on the other hand, is a real challenge. If you watch golf regularly you may have noticed that photographers never press the shutter until after the golfer hits the ball—otherwise the sound of a hundred shutters clicking

Pulling for focus *For shots like this, with crowd and hurdles nicely blurred, you must 'pull' the focus carefully to keep the moving athlete sharp*

simultaneously might put him off his stroke. In the normal course of events, then, there are little more than three basic golfing action shots—the follow-through on the tee shot, down on the fairway and in the bunker. It is possible to get good golfing shots, but it is far from easy.

Good swimming pictures are possibly even harder to come by since much of the action takes place below water—often all you can see is a slow moving head hidden beneath a black bathing cap. Certainly a row of swimmers plunging into the water at the start of a race can be spectacular, but everyone else shoots at the same moment!

Choose a sport with plenty of movement at first, and move on to the more awkward subjects when you have some experience behind you, unless you have a particular interest in an event.

Personal interest is certainly a big advantage because, if you know the game well, you will have a good idea where to stand to capture the heart of the action and you will know when to expect dramatic moments. If you know little about the sport you intend shooting, read up about it before the day. No more than a basic working knowledge is necessary—any more can lead to a tendency to take only obviously predictable shots.

Pro v. amateur

The glamour of professional sport acts like a magnet to photographers, and at any major event dozens of hopeful cameramen, both professional and amateur, are to be seen waiting around for the big moment. With so much competition, the chances of getting a good position to shoot from are not very high —even the professionals have problems. Most big venues have limits on the

Shooting football *With the grandstand out of focus, this superbly caught peak-of-the-action shot comes across strongly*

numbers of photographers they allow on the field and the chances of an amateur being given permission to sit on the pitch during a major football match or on the Centre Court at Wimbledon are extremely small.

Yet while the big names of sport make the headlines, they do not necessarily make good photographs. A tiny figure in the corner of the frame against a distracting background does not make a very exciting picture, even if the figure is a superstar—there are already thousands of bad pictures of any major personality. It is far better to get a good position at an amateur event than a bad position at a big professional game.

Many of the great sports pictures of history have been shot by amateurs at obscure events. There is always scope for pictures wherever you are. Because it is live action, there is always a chance of something unexpected happening whether you are at a Saturday kickaround or the Cup Final, and it is the element of surprise that makes sports photography exciting.

When it comes to the ideal range of equipment for sports photography no two people agree, because different situations require different treatment. At a tennis match, for instance, professionals shooting from the courtside tend to use a 135 mm lens for whole body shots up to the net and anything between 180 mm and 300 mm for baseline

Winter sports *With plenty of light, bright colours and an abundance of dramatic action, ski events offer tremendous scope for the photographer*

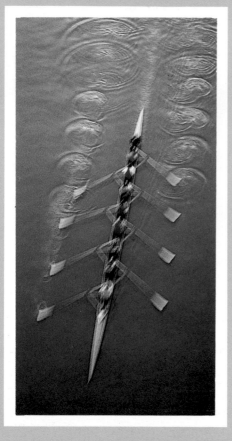

Rowing *Although fast action often needs rapid shutter speeds to stop movement, a slow shutter speed can blur the image to suggest pace very effectively*

Hang gliders *With so much colour and sparkle, sports like hang gliding make ideal subjects, but remember colour must be composed into a balanced picture*

Downfall of a cyclist *Sport is full of humour—keep your finger on the shutter ready for moments like this as well as the more obvious highspots*

Windsurfing *It is worth going to considerable lengths to get a good position to shoot from—here the photographer hired a boat*

Tennis *Up to the net volleys in tennis often provide dramatic moments. Look for signs of effort as the player returns —or fails to return—the ball*

Creating drama *Without thoughtful composition, the intense drama of the sports field can often be lost. While both of these pictures are pleasing, that on* *the left has more tension because the front runners, closer to the leading edge of the frame, seem to be straining to get out of the picture*

rallies. At a football match their choice would be completely different. Then, unfortunately, most amateurs do not have such freedom of choice.

You can get good results with virtually any camera and standard lens, given the right conditions, but probably the best combination is a basic 35 mm SLR with a 200 mm telephoto. The advantages of the telephoto over the standard lens are quite significant. A telephoto allows you to single out the interesting areas and blur out background distractions by

differential focusing. But above all it moves you right into the heart of the action so that you fill the frame with your subject. Anything bigger than 200 mm, though, would be unwieldy and difficult to use.

A zoom lens might seem an obvious choice for a sports photographer, providing a whole range of focal lengths and allowing him to switch his attention from one part of the field to another and still fill the frame. But most professionals use a zoom only for special effects or

when conditions restrict them to carrying a single lens. In normal conditions, a fixed focal length telephoto offers equivalent or superior performance and a wider maximum aperture for a given weight.

If you are using a telephoto, you will almost certainly need some sort of support for the camera. Hand held 200 mm shots can be taken, but the results are rarely completely sharp. A monopod —a one-legged version of a tripod—is probably the best solution. It is light, easy to carry, needs the minimum of space to erect and allows you complete freedom of movement with the camera, far more than a tripod with even the best pan-and-tilt head. Professionals find a monopod indispensable.

One other piece of equipment that may be useful though by no means essential, if you are keen on sports photography, is a motor drive for winding on the film automatically. Because in many sports the action happens so quickly, you have to keep your eye to the viewfinder all the time. Look away even for a second to wind on and you may miss a terrific picture. A motor drive solves this problem, though it can only be fitted to a camera designed to take one.

As for film, this depends on the weather conditions more than anything. The speed of the action tends to suggest a fast film for maintaining fast shutter speeds, but except in really gloomy conditions a fast film can be more of a nuisance than a help. Fast films tend to produce grainy results, and on a bright day they prevent you from opening the aperture to blur the background. In most conditions a fairly slow or medium speed

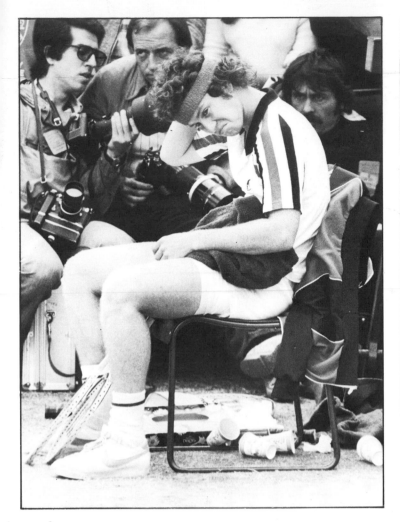

Exhaustion *It is the human element that often makes sports photographs—look out for the reactions of players in between the action*

film—in the range 64 to 100 ASA (ISO)—is fine, but in a fickle climate it is probably a good idea to take along a faster film—a 200 or even a 400 ASA in case the light closes in.

With continuous action on the field, there is a great temptation to shoot with a high shutter speed all the time. Although you can't go far wrong by doing this, it does not necessarily produce the most interesting pictures. It is true that high shutter speeds freeze the action and also allow you to use a wide aperture to isolate the subject against a blurred background. Indeed professionals tend to use high shutter speeds all the time because their pictures must be clear and 'artistic' effects are out of place—there is no such restriction on the amateur. Dramatic pictures with a tremendous amount of movement can be made by panning—following the subject in the viewfinder while taking the picture—with a slow shutter speed of 1/60 or even 1/30 second. This keeps the subject's body sharp, the limbs slightly blurred and the background an indistinct streak.

Too many panned shots, however,

Choosing the viewpoint *It is always worth looking for the unusual angle. Here a low viewpoint makes the horses loom over the camera dramatically*

Candid shots *If there is nothing happening on the field, there is often tremendous potential for candid shots among the crowd of spectators*

could become boring, and a good compromise shutter speed is 1/250 or 1/500 second which freezes most of the action while allowing just enough movement to give the picture a little life.

Blurring the background

While in most situations you can move your subject around, or move around your subject, to find a good background, in sports photography you are usually stuck with whatever happens to be behind the players. Invariably this is totally unsatisfactory—a crowd of spectators or an unsightly scoreboard, detracting from the main picture. The only way to overcome this is by using a wide aperture to keep the background out of focus.

But when the subject is moving about at high speed—and at worst is running towards you—it requires a lot of practice to get the hand-eye co-ordination just right so that you can 'pull' the focus as the subject bears down on you. Until you are absolutely sure of your ability to do this perfectly, it is probably better to shoot at $f/3.5$ or even $f/4$ rather than opening up all the way to $f/2.8$, if your lens allows it.

Deciding when to make the final commitment and press the shutter is largely a matter of experience. Once you have

been to a football match or an athletics meeting a few times you learn to anticipate moments of high drama. There are numerous highlights in tennis, for example, but an experienced sports photographer will be particularly wide awake when there are close-to-the-net volleys being played. There may be dynamic shots of players lunging for difficult returns or falling as they miss. But tennis is a very reactive sport and it is worth keeping your eyes open for emotional expressions between shots. One of the features to look for in all sports is signs of effort, not just in the face but in the whole body movement. The final result will look far more lively if the player seems to be really working. In tennis, this means that the best shots tend to come immediately after a player has made a stroke rather than before.

Every sport has its own set of standard 'peak of the action' pictures. They can be moves from set positions—the line-out in rugby or the service in tennis. Or they could be classic action shots of stars —Borg's backhand or Pele kicking the ball. Any number of shots of these situations have been taken. Professionals' files should be full of them, because they have to provide such basic shots for newspapers on demand. These pictures are visual clichés and it is a good idea to look for new situations for potential pictures. Look around for less obvious points of interest—a footballer does not need to have the ball at his feet to make an exciting picture.

Carnival time

A carnival or procession is a particularly rich and varied time for photographic opportunities, but planning and preparation can make a vast amount of difference to your pictures

Carnivals and processions, whether as elaborate as the Carnival in Rio de Janeiro, or as homely as a local May Day Parade, are all ideal occasions for photography. In one place and a short space of time, they offer colour, excitement, crowds and the special interest of the particular occasion—in short, a rich concentration of photographic opportunities. These displays and celebrations invariably have a strong visual content, so that there is normally no shortage of good material for the photographer, and this, together with the fact that every one involved expects to be photographed, makes them easy subjects for the camera.

With a large number of possible subjects—and different ways of treating them—you may even have some difficulty in choosing which to concentrate on. Although there is no need to limit yourself to just one aspect of a procession, it does help to know in advance exactly what the possibilities may be.

Although each carnival or procession naturally has its own special characteristics, there is usually one focal point to the event—the high point of the occasion. In a May Day Parade, it would be the May Queen, or in the City of London's Lord Mayor's Show, the carriage of the Lord Mayor himself. Under most circumstances, this would be the one subject that you would not want to miss, and it will usually be best to plan the rest of your coverage of the event around this.

For most photographers, however, the most exciting aspect of a parade is the opportunity to photograph people. On such an occasion, the people taking part in the celebration are deliberately putting themselves on display, and are animated and generally in high spirits. As a result, no-one has any reservations about being photographed, and the

Close-up *A telephoto is ideal for selecting one striking detail from the scene.* **Festival at Goa, India** *A strong shape makes an effective composition, while helping the subject to stand out against the background* **Carnival in Brazil** *Try to find a high viewpoint—local contacts can be very useful here* **Chinese Dragon Dance** *Going in close with a wide angle can give the flavour of being in the middle of the event*

common problems that you are likely to meet when photographing people in the street simply do not exist. Most participants are too involved in their parts to be shy or awkward in front of the camera.

This kind of event, in fact, makes an easy introduction to candid photography for anyone who feels embarrassed when aiming a camera at strangers: in a parade, nobody minds, and the success rate in terms of good poses and expressions is likely to be high.

The main difficulty with photographing people at a carnival or procession is that there is likely to be a large crowd of constantly moving bodies. Your pictures can easily turn out to be a dense and jumbled mass without a focal point, although what you actually thought you saw at the time may have been a clear view of a single float, costume, or group of people. Selective focusing may be one solution but people at these events are usually moving so quickly and unpre-

dictably that this may be difficult in practice. It may be best during a procession to focus on one spot and wait until people enter your focusing range. A zoom lens may help you to select particular details from the rest.

Alternatively, you can take the opposite approach and use a wide angle lens. This is useful in circumstances where you can move around and get close to your subjects. The wide angle allows you to use slower shutter speeds or to get

better depth of field than a telephoto, and can often help you to show all the action —maybe someone throwing flower petals into the crowd, for example. And a wide angle can often overcome distracting backgrounds by making them smaller in the frame.

Another valuable accessory in crowds is some means of shooting over people's heads. An aluminium camera case or even a wicker fishing basket can give you the extra height you need. Or you can hold the camera over your head and hope for a good aim, though in practice this can be tricky.

One aspect of processions that most casual photographers overlook is the preparation behind the scenes. People preparing and adjusting their costumes, lining up the order of the procession, or just relaxing with their feet up can provide some unusual views of the big day. By catching the participants off-guard, such as someone in elaborate historical costume lighting up a cigarette, you may have the chance of some candidly humorous moments. In addition, you may find that the way in which the procession is organized and rehearsed, and the details of how the floats, tableaux or decorations are actually constructed, are more interesting than the neat and ordered appearance in front of the public. Whether your photographs are printed and displayed, projected at a slide show, or even published, you will often find that, simply because of unfamiliarity, the audience will find this behind-the-scenes view particularly intriguing. For the annual Lord Mayor's Show in London, for example, few people know that the magnificent gold coach and full team of horses go through a dawn rehearsal in the deserted streets a few days before the event, with obvious pictorial possibilities. This may well happen in the case of other large events, and it would be worth finding out from the authorities concerned, so that you have a clear and uncluttered view of the proceedings.

Another subject to focus on is detail. Very often, people who photograph

Dancing figure *A fairly slow shutter speed, such as 1/30 second, captures the impressionistic effect of a fast moving dancer.* **Trinidad Carnival** *It is worth filling the entire frame with an extraordinary and colourful costume, such as this one*

colourful that a background of comparatively drab spectators can be a good visual contrast.

Of course, there is no need to restrict yourself to just one of these types of subject. Most parades and processions lend themselves well to a rounded, comprehensive treatment. By consciously trying to inject as much variety as possible into your coverage, you should be able to produce, by the end of the day, a successful picture essay. The essence of a picture essay is to cover all aspects of a subject, both in terms of content (the parade itself, preparations and costume details) and in pictorial variety with a combination of long shots, wide angle views, close-ups, subdued and strong colours. This naturally involves more concentration and more work, but the result, in which a selection of pictures balance each other, is generally worthwhile.

Having decided on how you are going to approach your parade in general terms, the key to success is your own planning and organization. This is because carnivals and parades are themselves usually organized quite tightly, so that your opportunities for photography are likely to occur in a short space of time, and in a limited area. Moreover, as these events invariably attract crowds, you will often find it difficult to move about—or even to get yourself into a suitable shooting

carnivals and processions concentrate on stepping back or fitting a wider angle lens to show an overall view of the event, ignoring the often intricate and elaborate costumes which can make subjects in themselves. Because processions are often organized on a fairly grand scale, and are usually seen quickly and not too closely, much of the detail gets lost, yet can be visually very attractive. In Rio's Carnival, for example, the costumes consume a great deal of effort and a sizeable proportion of the participants' yearly earnings, and would make a fascinating topic by themselves, apart from the dancing. On a less exotic level, the same often applies to carnivals nearer home. When concentrating on

costume you will find that one area of the outfit may be worth a specially detailed picture, even at the expense of the rest. An outrageous hat, waistcoat or shoes, or a tail pinned on to a child dressed up as a mouse, are possible subjects.

The spectators lining the route can themselves be subjects for photography, and as the parade passes, look for reaction shots among the crowd. Also be ready for any impromptu moments—this is generally a good situation for candid photography, as the spectators will be so caught up in watching the procession that you can often photograph people from only a metre or two without their noticing. The carnival or procession itself is likely to be so

Festival of Holi, India *These little girls, absorbed in the activities, were quite unaware of the camera.* **Profile** *This shot avoids the pitfall of a poor background by using a long lens at a wide aperture*

opportunity of shooting a particular part of the event. In all cases, check specifically the best places from which to shoot the type of pictures you have decided on. These sites are not always as obvious as you might imagine.

On many occasions, the closest spectator position to the focal point of the proceedings will be the most desirable, and if there is any special seating for dignitaries, or an enclosure for press photographers, this is where they will be located. However, such a position, which you will probably not be fortunate

position—once the parade is under way.

So, if you are going to take your photographic coverage seriously, you should work out your plan some days in advance. The first thing to do is to discover, as far as is possible, exactly what is going to happen, when, and where. In short, you need to know the programme, and for this, the best idea is to contact the organizers of the event (if you are in any doubt about who they are, the local tourist information office will normally be able to put you in touch). This is what a press photographer would do, and while there is no need to pretend that you are in competition with the professionals who are also covering the event, there is equally no reason for not giving yourself the same opportunity. Usually you will find that the organizers are helpful, and although you cannot expect them to give you a press pass and VIP treatment, they have a vested interest in publicizing their event, and so should welcome enquiries.

At the same time, if the event is an important or well-known one, look for any previously published photographs, in literature aimed at tourists, or in magazines such as *National Geographic*. This will give you some idea what type of event to expect. Armed with the schedule, you can then walk around the streets or park where the parade will take place, perhaps the day before the event. In the case of a carnival that moves along a route rather than stays in one place, check the timings, as it may be possible for you to move from one site to another in order to give yourself more than one

enough to get, may also carry hidden disadvantages. It may give the clearest view, but not necessarily the most interesting. Certainly, if you are at an event that has already been photographed countless times in previous years, your main concern will be to produce fresher images, probably from a new viewpoint. In addition, if you manage to find your way into a front-row seat, it may be very difficult to leave it halfway through to look for different shots.

Some less obvious positions may, with a suitable choice of lens, be more satisfactory. For instance, by standing to one side and using a wide angle lens it may be possible to include both the parade and spectators in one all-encompassing shot. Or, a position too distant for normal viewing might be ideal if you use a long telephoto lens. Be careful, however, with important events where security is likely to be tight. On the day, police often clear people away from some positions on public buildings and monuments.

A high viewpoint, such as an upper-storey window or the roof of an over-looking building, is often very suitable, allowing unrestricted views of a large area of the parade. With a wide angle lens you can take a scene-setting shot, while a telephoto lens gives a choice of selective close-ups. The disadvantage of a high position is that you may be stuck

Red and white *Sometimes there is no substitute for a front row position. A fast shutter speed freezes all the action.* **Festival in Spain** *A high viewpoint was essential here, as the viewer sees every face in the crowd and experiences the height of the act*

there for the duration of the parade, with little opportunity of moving around for different shots. With a procession, when the interesting parts may pass very very quickly, this type of position will often allow you only a few seconds to shoot a particular subject.

If you are feeling energetic, you could try, as an alternative, to work out a schedule that enables you to start with the preparations, as the participants arrive, dress, form up, and then move on to strategic viewpoints along the route that give a head-on view of the procession. This will almost certainly mean that you have to move fast, taking back routes between the streets that the procession is using. How much you will be able to move freely will, of course, depend on how crowded the route is

with spectators—there may be no problem at all with a local town parade, but at a major event the only solution is to arrive very early at the site and stay there.

Some of the places that you might want to photograph from may need special permission. If so, never be afraid to ask —you may be surprised at the help you receive. It is, however, important to make this kind of request in advance since the thing that really counts at these events is preparation and planning.

The equipment you take will obviously be influenced by what you intend to shoot, and where from. If you know that you are going to be in a fixed position, you might as well take as much equipment as you are likely to need—including a tripod, or a monopod, if space is very limited, as a useful and versatile support for a long focus lens. On the other hand, if your plan is to move quickly on foot, then you should take only what will fit easily into a shoulder bag. Wherever you shoot from, events will move rapidly to a peak and so a second camera body, already loaded with film, will help avoid missed shots.

Chapter 4
Landscapes
Composition

Brecon Beacons *The foreground detail in this panorama helps to lead the eye to the horizon*

The landscape is one of the classic themes in photography, and has attracted some of its greatest talents, including Ansel Adams, Edward Weston, and Bill Brandt. In fact, most photographers, whatever their speciality, have come to grips with the landscape at some time or another. Landscapes are such accessible subjects, and there is something in human nature that is attracted to broad, sweeping views, so that they have a universal appeal in photography.

The landscape, however, can mean different things to different people. Everyone would agree that a vista from a vantage point is a landscape, but virtually any view which involves features at some distance can be thought of as a landscape. In general there should not be too many man-made elements in the view, otherwise the scene becomes an urban landscape. Neither should it consist of largely nearby objects which dominate the picture. Thus a picture of a

barn is not a landscape, even if distant hills are visible at one side, while a scene in which the barn is seen in its surroundings from a distance very probably is a landscape, even though the distant hills may not be included.

In approaching landscape photography, composition is one of the most crucial factors, since it is one of the few variables that is under the photographer's direct control. Landscapes are essentially static subjects, and this fact limits the ways in which you can introduce an individual interpretation to the image. Landscapes do change—with the season and the weather—but so slowly that within the time that most people spend on a photograph, they present a virtually fixed appearance. While lighting is usually a major variable, in the

case of landscape, it is beyond control. Although a dedicated landscape photographer may find the time to wait until the lighting conditions are just right, most people cannot, and have to work with the conditions as they find them. This leaves composition as one of the principal ways in which a photographer can interpret a landscape according to his or her tastes and ideas.

Composition is simply the arrangement of the graphic elements of an image so it is enhanced or it creates a deliberate impression. Unfortunately, it suffers from having been treated too often as an abstract theory, rather than as a part of practical photography. In practice, every photograph is composed —just the act of pointing the camera selects and organizes the components of the picture—and whether this composition is deliberate, intuitive, or even unwitting, it is a vital factor in the power of the image. Since landscapes are fixed

division exact, the principle is that the ratio of the smaller section to the larger should be the same as that of the larger section to the whole. In practice, dividing a line or rectangle in the proportions 5:8 or 3:5 is about right.

A great deal of nonsense has been written about the Golden Section, mainly by people who feel that it is a rule that must be adhered to. It is nothing of the sort. Simply, it is an observation from the experience of many painters and photographers that most people find to be an aesthetically pleasing way of dividing up a picture. In practice, most people tend to compose images this way without consciously thinking about it. If a satisfactory landscape composition, with nothing out of the ordinary, is what you want, then by all means arrange the horizon and other elements according to

Farmland *Here the shot has been framed to concentrate on the colour and depth created by the seed rows*

Stone walls *The interest lies in the curved lines picked out by the high viewpoint and long lens. Compare this approach with the* **New Forest dawn,** *in which a 28 mm lens and low viewpoint required the photographer to balance the foreground with the background tree*

and so allow you time to work, they permit more careful composition than most subjects.

In photography, as in painting and drawing, the elements of an image that can be altered are points, lines and shapes. However, the simple, two-dimensional patterns that these make are overlaid in any photograph by the significance of the subject itself. For instance, imagine a desert view where a thin strip of road in the distance is the only distinguishable feature. If a car appears on that road, it will be extremely small in the frame—too small under

ordinary circumstances to affect the composition. However, a solitary car in extremely barren surroundings immediately becomes the focus of attention. In this way, composition in photography has to take into account the interest of the different elements as well as their graphic appearance.

Most textbook discussions on composition focus on a system of proportion usually called the Golden Section. This is a way of dividing lines and the frame of the picture so as to give what is generally thought of as a pleasing composition. Although you do not have to make the

the Golden Section—but it is more important that you use the composition to draw attention to the features that you find important.

The first thing to consider when composing a landscape photograph, which is often overlooked because it is so obvious, is the format of the picture. Most broad views are essentially horizontal—the horizon line takes care of that—and these generally suit the horizontal 35 mm format that most people use. The same 35 mm frame used vertically, does not work in most landscape subjects because the eyes do not find it as easy to scan up and down as they do from side to side. But, the subject needs some vertical components, to break up the horizontal lines, such as trees or mountains, to be successful. A square format is probably the most difficult of all to compose within, and most landscape photographs taken on 6 × 6 cm cameras tend to be cropped for display. A panoramic format, on the other hand, suits many horizontal land-scapes very well—the proportions, generally about 3:1, make it possible to eliminate a featureless foreground or sky, and allows you to concentrate on the landscape itself.

As most landscape photographs in-clude a horizon line, and as this is often very distinct, positioning it in the frame becomes one of the main decisions in composition. It often divides the picture into two definite areas, and so the Golden Section is frequently relevant. In the absence of any unusual features, the most natural way of placing the horizon is roughly a third of the way up from the bottom edge of the frame—in other words, according to the Golden Section. The result is satisfactory rather than remarkable, but is nearly always better than a straight half-and-half composition, with the horizon in the exact middle. This type of division is so obviously regular that it can easily create a dull, rather uninspiring image.

Prairie landscape *Placing the horizon low in the frame and allowing the sky to dominate creates a feeling of wide open space.*
Stenness stones *Two separate points of interest have produced a shot which actually benefits from a central horizon*

However, if you tilt the camera so that you move the horizon to the bottom of the frame, the possibilities can be much more interesting. This type of composition naturally gives more emphasis to the sky (which may deserve it because of interesting cloud formations), but it also gives a strong feeling of weight and solidity, and at the same time an open, unrestricted feeling. For an expansive view of rolling grassland or prairie, this might be ideal—and, incidentally, a good solution for a featureless foreground.

By placing the horizon at the very top of the frame, you have yet another approach. This can give the shot quite a different feel. Since the camera points down, it can give an introspective or even closed in feel. The viewer's attention is not drawn immediately to the top of the picture, and you may be able to make good use of this if you have an unusual subject on the horizon. The viewer's eye tends to notice it only after a delay, which means that you have introduced an element of surprise quite successfully.

With some views, however, particularly those from a high viewpoint with a long focus lens, the horizon may be a distraction, taking attention away from the more interesting elements in the landscape. If so, it is better left out of the frame altogether.

Once you have decided on your main reasons for shooting the picture, look objectively at your subject and choose one of the components of the scene which will produce the most effective result. This is not as easy as it sounds since, with a landscape, your senses often override what the eye sees. So your general impression is just as likely to be influenced by mood, sound, smells, and even memories, as by purely visual information. But the camera lens will record the scene quite objectively and may well record things that your eyes may have glossed over, such as barbed wire fences or pylons. One way of training your eyes to be objective is to literally put a frame around the subject—you could use your hands or make a cardboard frame. Try to identify the components of the scene. In your landscape these may consist of a line of distant hills, a field of wheat, a river, and a building at the foot of the hills for instance. The next consideration is the relationship between these various elements in terms of shape and size. Determine which of the elements really contributes to the picture, and which detracts from it.

Many good landscape photographs contain a single element that is the main focus of interest—something that, by virtue of its colours, tone, shape or recognizability, attracts immediate atten-

tion. It might be a solitary rock on the horizon, a distant river glinting in late afternoon sunlight, or one flowering tree in a forested valley. Knowing that it will catch the eye if included in the picture, you should place it in the frame so that it relates easily to the rest of the composition. Usually, an off-centre position works best—placing it centrally would be a little unimaginative, whereas placing it close to the frame edge tends to be distracting and can appear careless.

Often, however, a landscape usually contains more than one strong element, so that the composition must reconcile different points of interest. Two strong features will tend to fight for attention—in a coastal scene, for example, with a white house on the shore and a lighthouse on a headland, the eye will shuttle to and fro between them. Occasionally, this can make the image more dynamic. If the effect you want is of a placid view, then it is something to be avoided, but at other times it can be valuable. For instance, you might want to point out a relationship between the large view of a landscape—mountains, rivers and fields—and its small components—grass, flowers, small rocks. In such a case, you should look

Trees in mist *In this almost monochrome landscape, a 300 mm lens picked out the trees emerging from the mist but left out the foreground*

Bryce Canyon *When composing a landscape it is not always a good idea to try and include a wide view. This study of the rock formations in Bryce Canyon, Utah, shows the value of concentrating on special features*

Monochrome landscape *Black and white film allows the photographer to concentrate on shape and light— like these hills and the dramatic sky*

Field patterns *Another approach to composing landscapes is to exclude the horizon and any other clues which would destroy the abstract effect*

Stile *The line of hills is interesting, but does not fill the frame. A stile is a good foreground object, as its nature leads the eye into the picture*

specifically for two points of interest: one in the distance and one in the foreground. A wide angle lens is very useful in this style of composition, or with a view camera, you can use tilts or swings to bring both near-foreground and horizon into focus together.

An extension of this foreground– background technique is to provide a natural frame for a distant subject. There is no need to look for something as specific as a rock arch, although these can provide very good creative opportunities when you can find them, but the overhanging branches of a tree, or a mountainside gully seen from above can be just as useful. The effect of a natural frame, which usually works best when it is darker than the scene beyond it, is to

focus attention more strongly and to reduce the importance of the rectangular picture border. It does, however, need to be used judiciously, as there is a danger of cliché.

Choice of lens has a significant effect on landscape composition, and in this, photography differs from traditional painting. Focal length, from very wide angle to telephoto, imposes its own graphic rules on the image. Wide angle views tend to show the broad sweep of a landscape emphasizing, at the same time, details close to the camera. The perspective effect of a short focal length lens exaggerates the size of foreground objects, making it possible to integrate in one photograph a detail, such as a flower, with the structure of the landscape in the distance. Also, because of this wide angle of view, such lenses nearly always show the horizon, making conscious control over the position of the horizon line important.

A long focal length, on the other hand, produces a magnified view of one small area, and creates foreshortening. Both of these qualities make it possible to compose with a telephoto lens in a graphic and sometimes abstract way. By moving the lens only slightly, the arrangements of shapes and lines can be changed significantly, while the flatter perspective gives a more two-dimen-

sional image. If you want to make a set of variations in composition, a long focus lens is the most useful additional item of equipment you can have.

Choice of viewpoint is directly linked to composition. From a low viewpoint, the horizon nearly always appears in the image, and usually has to be placed in the lower part of the frame, while a high viewpoint—looking down on a landscape from a clifftop, for example—gives wider choice. From any given camera position, you can work to improve the composition, but you will probably find that altering your viewpoint slightly can help immensely.

What sets a successful landscape photograph apart from a stereotyped postcard view is the appreciation of which components make the view interesting and the ability to emphasize these. Composition is your chief control in doing this: if it is the expanse of sky over an open prairie that you find appealing, then a low horizon line will help convey this feeling, while if the dominant feature is a row of foothills receding into haze, then a selective view with a telephoto lens may help, eliminating everything except the pattern of ridges, one on top of the other.

Always make composition serve your needs, drawing attention to the parts of the image that you consider important.

Water

Whether the subject is a magnificent lake at sunset or a street puddle in the pouring rain, water can be an impressive element to include in your photographs

Industrial scene *By including such a large expanse of water in the foreground the photographer has avoided concentrating too much upon a mirror image. The evening light produced colour in the still water*

Swimming pool *The patterns of the sunlight reflected in the water and the way the water distorts the squared tiles on the pool floor produced striking results. Often it is worthwhile showing just water, leaving out all else*

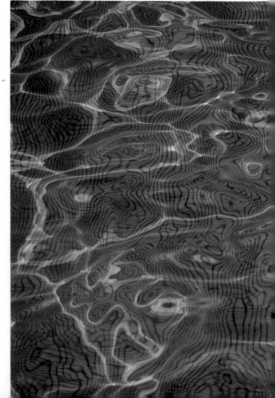

Water is a subject which fascinates everybody. People will stare for hours into a lazily meandering river, walk long distances to see waterfalls, and delight in the babbling of a mountain brook. After all, water is vital to life, and it can take so many forms, appearing at times black and forbidding, and at others blue and sparkling. It is when you come to view your pictures of it that the magic sometimes disappears.

Photographing water successfully is partly a matter of technique, but it is even more important to think creatively. You must use all the skill you have to capture in a still picture something which is essentially dynamic and liquid.

Think, for example, of a waterfall. The beginner will simply click the shutter at some average speed, but the more experienced photographer will make a decision at this point—is it best to 'freeze' the water with a rapid shutter speed, or to allow it to flow for a long exposure ? In practice, if you are close

enough for the water droplets to be seen, the best results are obtained at speeds of either 1/250 and faster, or 1/8 and slower. Anything in between tends to look rather like rice pudding. For the longer speeds, a neutral density filter may be needed to cut down the light sufficiently, even at the smallest aperture.

Having made this decision about the appearance of the water, you can now start to think about the rest of the picture. If the surroundings are attractive there seems little problem ; but quite often the result is a straightforward pretty picture, with little real originality. It may even be unsatisfactory, because all the ingredients were there but somehow the picture seems lopsided. There is often a problem of balance with waterfall pictures—you have restricted access, and there may be deep shadows which create disturbing black areas. The waterfall, seen from a bank, tends to fill one side of the picture with nothing on the other side to balance it. Alternatively, if you are looking more or less square on to it, it becomes two-dimensional.

To deal with these problems, you should obviously move around as much as possible. Some of the best shots appear with the light behind the water: any dark shadows may then be filled with glinting droplets or spray. A hint of soft focus or flare may not be out of place. Look round for objects in the foreground or background that will either create compositional problems or will fill black holes. It may even be necessary to view the waterfall between fronds of foliage to make it appear to be in a leafy glade—even if it is surrounded by unattractive steps or is largely in shadow.

The bigger waterfalls, up to Niagara size, can be surprisingly difficult to photograph. There is less of a problem with shutter speed, as the water is too distant to show much detail, but people often make the mistake of trying to get everything into the picture, with the result that the waterfall itself is lost between the foreground and the sky. Niagara itself is a case in point. It is a very popular tourist attraction, but access is more or less restricted to viewpoints on either bank. Most pictures of it look rather similar and rather boring.

The amazing thing about Niagara is its sheer size—but this is usually lost in photographs. A good way to show the scale would be to use a long focus lens— probably around 300 mm—to take close-ups of the falls and spray. With such a large image scale, shutter speed again becomes a problem, but with the lens at full aperture you can probably use 1/125 on a fine day even on fairly slow film.

Another way of showing the scale of such a huge waterfall is to include some suitable object near to or in the disturbed water. Small boats often take tourists close to the falls, but are not

Brazilian waterfall *Large waterfalls are very difficult to photograph—you have to find a good viewpoint and resist the urge to include the entire scene*

permitted to move sufficiently close for you to include them in a long focus shot from the banks. By taking a boat trip yourself, you may be able to take a dramatic shot with another boat in the foreground. A moderately long focal length will compress the distance and make the other boat appear to be virtually underneath the falls. Again you may not be able to choose a fast enough shutter speed, particularly if you are on board a boat yourself, unless you use a fast film.

More isolated waterfalls often present fewer difficulties of access, but you must still strive to show the scale and fill awkward spaces in your composition. Including a figure is an obvious way of showing the scale—you could either take the long focus lens approach, which would mean retreating some distance away, or go to the other extreme and use a wide angle lens from a low viewpoint, with both the figure and the falls towering over you. Both approaches will help to make the falls fill the frame.

Larger falls, where there is plentiful spray around, often have attractive rainbows. You must look for these with the sun behind you—they are seen at an angle of 42° from your shadow, so you will probably need to look down on the spray. A polarizing filter may help to make the rainbow clearer.

Close-ups of falls, whether large or small, also benefit from careful composition. As always, the simpler compositions are usually the more effective so a comparatively long focal length is useful to avoid having to move too close to the water.

The same approach is valuable when you are photographing a stream or small swift-flowing river, with plenty of rocks to impede its progress. Little eddies and splash points can be isolated to capture the feel of movement where an overall shot might be too confusing. Shooting from a very low viewpoint, if you can manage it, may help to compress the

ripples on the water surface to emphasize its flowing nature.

Where the river gets wider, its surface becomes much more bland and uninteresting, and it is often more worthwhile to take the overall view, looking at the shape of the river in the landscape. Running water has a major effect on the landscape, carving and moulding it, so the wide view can be quite revealing.

On a smaller scale, shots taken along the river bank, concentrating on the water, work particularly well if you use reeds or foliage as a frame. Sun glinting on the water is something of a cliché, but you can still find new ways of looking at it by moving in close, using reeds as a frame as if you were some water creature looking to see if the coast is clear. An effects filter, such as a starburst, can be useful; you can often obtain starburst effects without one if you stop your lens down to a small aperture, which is often essential in any case. If you follow the meter's reading, the picture will look rather dark with just a few highlights, so the thing to do is to overexpose by about a stop, or to take the meter reading from an area nearby but without the brilliant glints of light and then lock the exposure on that reading.

Lakes can also prove to be difficult subjects unless you are far enough away from them to photograph an overall view. From the water's edge they appear as large and possibly bland expanses, which turn out to be rather featureless in the final result. Again, natural frames are useful; long focus lenses used looking across the water surface can compress what features there are; and wide angle lenses can turn broad bands of water, hills and sky into semi-abstracts. It may also be worthwhile subduing nearby reflections so that you can see details below the surface in the foreground, such as weed or rocks, to add interest.

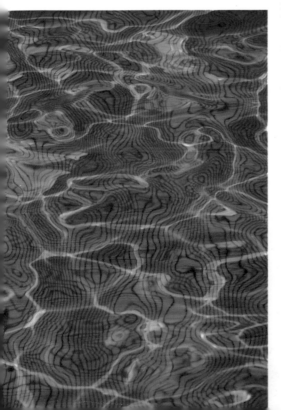

Oily river *Often there is potential subject matter floating on the surface of water. Here the photographer noticed the way the oily trail curved around the plant and framed the shot to concentrate on this small detail.* **Walking in the wet** *After a fall of rain a city can take on a new look..In this shot the reflections make the vertical lines of the building continue down the full length of the frame creating a striking graphic effect which makes an impressive framework for positioning the people.* **Forest dawn** *A mysterious atmosphere has been established by photographing this scene in the early morning mist, highlighted by the sun. The water in this shot has mirrored the undergrowth, emphasizing the density of the forest.* **Wet close-up** *By closing in on the water droplets clinging to these blades of grass, the photographer has produced an intriguing, almost abstract image. Shots like this usually work best when photographing the subject against the light.* **Java salt pan** *Water always multiplies the effects of dramatic skies—the two together also create a bright background that lends itself to framing a scene with a silhouetted subject. A graduated filter has added colour to the almost mono-chrome scene of the salt worker. The exposure reading was taken from the brighter areas of the scene to create the silhouette*

Waterfall *The fundamental decision which has to be made when photographing a waterfall is that of shutter speed and whether or not you want to freeze the movement of the water or create a milky blur. Here a slow speed has made the water look like a strange, formless mass, contrasting with the hard shapes of the surrounding rock.*
Fountain *In contrast, a faster shutter speed has been used for this shot so that the water issuing from the fountain has made trails in mid air. For best effect, a shot like this should be composed so that the trails of water are backlit*

background of lake or river. Make sure that you expose for the lighter water or sky areas so that you achieve a dark silhouette in the foreground.

Early morning and evening are also times when you may catch mist rising from the water. This may be a positive advantage if you want to create a moody or mysterious picture with delicately muted colours and tones. If the mist is strong enough to obliterate most of the colour, this may be an opportunity to use a graduated colour filter to bring colour to the sky area, so that the water contrasts with it.

Water can take on a remarkably different appearance in different seasons. Rain on the surface of a lake or pond can result in a fractured, moving and glistening surface which can be photographed using different shutter speeds for very interesting effects. Do not overlook the modest puddle at this time. It can provide you with a fascinating series of reflections, particularly at night when splashes of light can be seen in its surface. Try using a slow shutter speed so that colours 'swirl' together.

Perhaps the most extreme change that water undergoes is in winter when it freezes. At this time you can make the most of a monochrome landscape in the background with a frozen lake as the centre of interest, or you can choose to

Reflections themselves, on the other hand, can be one of the main attractions of water for the photographer. The precise mirror images given by calm water are certainly beautiful to the eye, but do not always retain quite their initial attraction. One way round this is simply to photograph the surface of the water so that you avoid the repetition of the double image. Or, if the water is broken up by ripples, go for a more impressionistic effect, with only part of the actual image present in the picture. Some of the most spectacular reflections can be seen when you are looking across water towards a low sun from a fairly high viewpoint. Use a telephoto lens to achieve a really dramatic effect. Occasionally the reflected image is so broken up as to be completely unrecognizable, and you can concentrate on the abstract qualities of pattern and colour instead. As the water ripples depend on the breeze, the shape of the reflection changes a great deal, and you may find, in a comparatively short time, that you have a whole series of different pictures taken from the same patch of water.

The time of day and the type of weather can alter the appearance of any kind of water most dramatically. Late evening, in particular, can transform a dull waterside scene into a romantic or mysterious image simply by the quality of the light. A dull, muddy river might become a bright ribbon of gold while a tiny pool can be turned into a patch of light bringing relief to dark, rolling hills and a menacing sky. The colours of the sky may be richly saturated, re-

flecting into the water, and cloud formations may be lit from below, giving vivid reflections.

Evening light can pick up every detail and ripple in the water, and it may be worth exploiting these effects with the help of a telephoto lens. Use any foreground details in the late afternoon and evening, especially silhouettes which can provide a positive contrast to a

exploit colour contrast, using brightly dressed children skating on the ice as a contrast to the white surface of the water. Whether it is spring or autumn, do not overlook colourful blossom or dead leaves which may have fallen into the water from adjacent bushes and trees. When photographed at close range, these provide bright contrasts with the tones of the water on the bed below.

Woods and trees

Woods and trees can be very rewarding subjects for the photographer, offering a wealth of material, from close-ups to a general view

To the photographer out and about with a camera, trees always seem obvious and attractive subjects. Abundant over much of the world, full of subtle colour and detail, conveniently sized and endowed with a pleasingly complete natural shape—and obligingly still when posing. They could be made for the photographer and given the right exposure any shot should be attractive. Yet results rarely live up to expectations, disappointing in both shape and colour, so for successful tree photographs, you must apply a little thought and imagination before setting up a shot.

One of the problems is that precisely because of the profusion of detail and the subtle coloration, the complex outlines of trees are often lost against anything but the plainest of backgrounds. Where-ever there is any strong detail in the background, the outlines of trees become indistinct and the result is rather flat. This is not always obvious when you take the picture because, with normal stereoscopic vision, you can see the scene in depth. In a two dimensional photograph, it is not instantly clear what detail belongs to the tree in the foreground and what to the background. Other trees make particularly bad backgrounds in this respect.

Paradoxically, then, forests and heavily wooded countryside are often the hardest places to photograph trees effectively and, if you want a clear outline, it is better to look for isolated copses in open country, or even the city. Indeed, lone trees, particularly those that are exceptionally large and elegant, often make the best photographs. But the surrounding landscape must be very simple for this type of shot to work.

Look carefully for a viewpoint that gives a clear uncluttered background, or a background so distant that its soft colour and detail do not distract. A few large trees standing in smoothly rolling grassy fields or parkland make effective shots, especially when a low angle sun casts long shadows on the grass, revealing all the gentle undulations but disguising most of the detail.

Where the landscape is too full of detail or too similar in tone to the tree you could try shooting against the sky. The general outline of the tree and even individual leaves and branches should stand out clearly against the bright pure tone of the sky. If you are shooting trees against the sky, be careful that not only

Crowning glory *Do not always look for pictures at eye level. In a thin wood, shoot directly overhead with a wide angle lens to get a spoke effect*

Fungus *In the soft light from a cloudy sky, close ups of bark texture and parasitic growth can be effective.*

the topmost branches project above the horizon—unless the landscape is light in tone, the full outline of the tree is lost and the impact of the shot is reduced. To achieve a complete outline, you may have to adopt a low viewpoint even in fairly flat country, or find a tree or copse on the crest of a ridge.

An interesting approach is to work the shot so that the character of the tree and the sky match or complement each other. An old gnarled tree with withered, twisted branches could be shot against a stormy sky with swirling clouds; a light feathery tree could be pictured against a sky full of feathery cirrus clouds or against a pale sunset. Often the character of the landscape will enhance this effect because the tree is adapted to its environment.

Establishing the correct exposure for shots against the sky can be difficult because trees are generally much darker than the sky. In the photograph, either the tree is rendered too darkly or the sky is washed out. There is no easy solution to this problem and it is worth making more bracketed exposures than normal to ensure satisfactory results.

Try to avoid shooting with the sun beyond the tree, unless you want to create a silhouette. Strong sunlight from behind the camera, on the other hand, minimizes the difference in tone between the tree and the sky but may not necessarily produce the best results.

With large, full-leafed deciduous trees, strong direct sunlight washes out the colour in the leaves and gives so little shadow that the rounded form of the body of the tree is completely flattened. This kind of tree really needs oblique lighting, preferably from a fairly low angle, to give solidity of form. With more spindly trees, however, or when the branches are bare in winter, strong direct sunlight can turn the bark to an almost silvery white that looks very effective against a deep blue sky.

Perhaps the best approach, though, is to throw the tree or copse into silhouette. Again, silhouettes tend to be more effective with bare branched trees which form a dark tracery against the sky or, alternatively, if you close in on a single bough so that individual leaves are almost visible.

Remember that there is no need for the tree to fill the frame like a full length portrait. Because of its complex outline and detail, a tree can be the focus of attention even if it only occupies a small area of the frame. A popular approach is to photograph a very simple open landscape with just a single tree or a small copse on the horizon. Providing there is little detail in the foreground—it could be snow covered or simply grassy—the tree will attract the eye. Indeed, you could make an almost abstract composition by using a tele-photo and the vertical format to give the picture just three elements—the plain foreground field, the middle distance tree and the sky. With few clues to depth, the appearance is almost abstract.

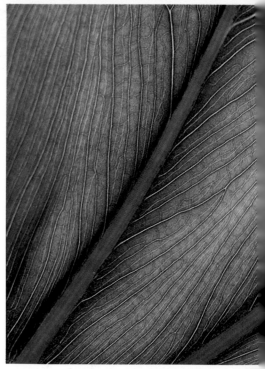

Autumn colours *In thin woodland, you can shoot through clumps of trees, exploiting colour contrasts between bark and leaves.* **Leaf** *Extreme close-ups take the viewer into a world in which objects appear very differently. Here backlighting shows up each tiny vein.* **Sunset** *Evening is an excellent time to photograph trees, especially against a dramatic sky—a break in the clouds helps trees to stand out clearly.* **Woods in snow** *Most trees and woods take on a completely different look each season, but especially during the winter when dark trees provide a strong contrast to the white ground*

An isolated copse in the distance, on the other hand, can provide an effective key point for atmospheric landscapes in dramatic lighting conditions.

With their very distinct characteristics, trees benefit from contrasts. You can contrast green palm branches or dark branches with a blue sky, but look for contrasts between types of trees as well. In heavy coniferous woods, look for a few isolated clumps of light deciduous trees. From a distance—perhaps the other side of a valley—the big deciduous trees stand out clearly against the dark and heavy textured conifers.

Contrasts with rock surfaces or buildings may be equally effective. In cities, the organic shape and subtle colouring of trees nicely complements the angularity and harsh colours of modern buildings.

Of course, there is no need to photograph single trees or stands—although their outlines are strong and distinctive, trees offer many other photographic possibilities. An avenue of tall, elegant trees, for instance, provides a gentle, pleasing pattern if you shoot down the length of a row, capturing the repetition of the trunks. The slender trunks of young trees, shot against the light, give a similarly attractive pattern, particularly if the shot includes a few bright, almost flared highlights.

Where the trees are slender and there are few leaves on the trees—in spring or winter—there are many interesting patterns to be found if you try shooting from all kinds of unusual viewpoints. One approach that is often effective is to lie on your back and point the camera up at the crowns of the trees. With a wide angle lens fitted on the camera, the trunks of the trees seem to converge sharply towards the tops, creating a dynamic spoke-like effect. If you can, include the sun in the frame and

shoot with a narrow aperture, so that the sun's rays seem to positively burst through the trees.

Trees respond more than most subjects to changing lighting conditions and it is worth returning to the same spot again and again to exploit the changes. In light woodland, early morning and late afternoon often give the most interesting lighting possibilities—at least when the sun is shining. Sunlight penetrates beneath the eaves of the wood at a low angle, sidelighting the trunks and picking out small areas of foliage.

When the sun is higher, light penetrates the leaf cover less easily and gives dappled, confused lighting which rarely looks as good on film as it did in reality.

However, when a few shafts of sunlight pierce thick foliage, the effects can be quite dramatic. Shooting into the sun in these conditions produces dark shadows and brilliant highlights.

Of course lighting effects vary from wood to wood and from season to season. In winter in deciduous woodland, the trees are bare and there is less to stop the light reaching the woodland floor. This, then, is often the best time to make close-up studies, particularly when you have a clear view of a single leaf, exposed root or interesting bark texture. A layer of frost can make even the dullest leaf stand out and sparkle, especially when backlit.

In deciduous woodlands, each season

has its own interest. New growth in spring, rich foliage in summer, strong colours in autumn and a more open view in winter. If you have easy access to a forest or wood you can chart the passage of the seasons by photographing the same scene from the same position at different times of the year.

With such an abundance to photograph, and conditions that change noticeably in appearance, woods are ideal locations for working on one of the most interesting of all photographic projects—a picture essay. Instead of concentrating on individual images, you can construct, over a period of time, a variety of photographs around a central theme like autumn colour.

Silhouette *If a tree has an unusual or interesting shape, you could wait for the right conditions for a silhouette. In this shot strange colouring suits the gnarled, twisted outline.* **Tree and building** *In the city, look for the contrasts between trees and buildings in shape, colour and texture. Here the photographer has used a telephoto lens to draw tree and building closer together, framing tightly so that the most interesting part of the tree is seen without any distractions from the street.* **Tree and sheep** *An almost perfectly symmetrical composition suits a tree which has a similarly symmetrical design, while a careful composition balances horizon and sky in a clean line.* **Fallen leaves** *In autumn, leaves on the ground can make attractive pictures, particularly early in the season. But move around and choose your viewpoint to include a few leaves of contrasting colours— or even arrange the leaves yourself.* **Early morning mist** *In fairly open rolling countryside, isolated clumps of trees can make effective shots, particularly early in the day when the low angle sun picks out the small undulations in the ground and mist softens outlines and obscures back- grounds. Remember to use texture lines such as furrows or tracks to lead the eye towards the subject*

Anyone visiting the tropics is presented with spectacular scenery that just cries out to be photographed. But when you are back home, sorting through the shots, there are dozens of beautiful pictures—virtually all the same. The stunning scenery tends to bemuse the photographer, whose creative skills seem redundant. Just press the button and you have a classic shot. But if you want shots that are different from those of every other holidaymaker, you must try as hard as ever to be original. This means exploiting the conditions that are peculiar to the tropics.

The tropics do have a special flavour which sets them apart from any other area—a direct result of their particular location straddling the equator. The sun rises rapidly and almost vertically, and at midday it is directly overhead for part of the year. Outside the tropics it is never quite so high. Consequently, one type of natural light that is exclusively tropical occurs in the middle of the day when shadows lie directly underneath objects and everything else is bathed in a harsh glare.

With a large scale subject such as a landscape, there are virtually no shadows visible. While this flat lighting gives little in the way of modelling, there are ways of using it attractively. It does, in any case, help to convey some sense of the great heat that the tropics experience.

Scenes that have marked differences

Tropical landscapes

Like most successful landscape photography, taking creative shots in the tropics involves making use of the interesting and unusual features peculiar to the region

in tone or colour, and views that have strong, well-defined shapes, generally photograph well under high sunlight such as this. The very flatness of the lighting often helps to emphasize those outlines and colours which are not obscured by prominent shadows. A beach, for example, offers strong graphic images consisting of bold splashes of colour from the rich blues and greens set against white sand.

Similarly, in desert areas where the colour of sand and rock is not obscured by any vegetation, and where rock formations often weather into interesting shapes, the middle of the day is a good time to compose images that have abstract qualities. If you want to exploit

these effects fully, try underexposing slightly to saturate the colours. A careful choice of viewpoint helps to clarify and emphasize a particular structure or shape in the landscape, ensuring, perhaps, that a pale background sets off the shape of a darker tree or foreground feature.

Another advantage of high sun is that a polarizing filter has a very pronounced effect, particularly on a blue sky close to the horizon. The strong blue resulting can be used creatively to provide a dramatic background for a tropical landscape.

At any other time of the day you must be prepared to work quickly where the light is an important element because the

Hillside *In this landscape, the patch of sunlight creates a warm area of green to contrast with the stormy sky*

sun rises and sets in tropical areas much more quickly than it does in temperate zones. The sun rises and sets almost vertically and can be captured on film by using a very long time exposure. Using a slow film, small aperture and several neutral density filters (giving a density of about 4), you will find that you can extend an exposure, even of a low sun, to several minutes. If you use a telephoto lens, you can concentrate on one small section of the sky fairly close to the horizon. You will see that the image of the sun appears to move very quickly in the viewfinder, so you should begin the exposure just as the sun comes into view at the top of the frame. This will result in nothing but a vertical line as the sun sets, so during twilight uncover the lens again for a second or so to expose some landscape details on the same frame.

Tropical twilight often has very unusual colouring, which you can photograph quite easily with time exposures of a few seconds. The only problem is

Sunset *A telephoto is often best for catching a setting sun—it magnifies the size of the orb and silhouettes gain more impact.* **Palm trees** *This picture was taken at dawn, when the lack of wind allowed a long exposure time*

that the palm trees which often form an important part of such a scene will move in the breeze if more than a brief exposure is used. One solution to this problem may be to photograph the dawn sky, when the wind may be less

Tropical weather brings its own variations, often dramatic, to both the light and the landscape itself. Although bright sunlight seems to typify the tropical day, the weather conditions that strong, particularly near the coast. are actually unique to the tropics are the storms and rain. Depending on the season and on the actual location in the

Rock *Shooting straight into the sun can give a sense of heat as well as enhancing the shape of the main subject*

tropics, one of the most memorable sights is that of an afternoon storm building up. Tropical areas receive so much heat during the day that they experience quite regular late afternoon rain which is often accompanied by a storm. The resulting thunderclouds make impressive additions to a landscape photograph, and usually cause violent but brief rainstorms which bring dramatically changing conditions, often clearing completely by sunset.

Since these convectional storms cover several kilometres of altitude, their aftermath is frequently a sky scattered with many different types of cloud, and it is this, more than anything else, that makes tropical sunsets so interesting. These cloud formations can disperse very quickly, so it is a good idea to find a clear view over the countryside well in advance of the predicted storm, and wait for the weather conditions to develop. The comparative predictability of the weather makes this easier in the tropics than in temperate latitudes.

Night storms are typical in some tropical areas, but are not as easy to photograph. They are best photographed with high speed film, as the clouds are usually dense, withholding much of the illumination from the lightning. In these cases mount your camera on a tripod, use a fast lens at maximum aperture, and leave the shutter open until one or more flashes of lightning have occurred in the direction your camera is pointing.

Parts of the South East Asian tropics experience another, very specific, weather condition—the monsoon. In its most extreme form it brings continuous,

Empty beach *A polarizer helps to intensify the colours and underline the tropical flavour of a scene*

Stepped fields *Unusual features are well worth photographing—here the palm tree adds extra interest*

torrential rain, and while for general photography it can pose great practical difficulties, it can occasionally make very impressive photographs. It is not a season to recommend for a visit, but if you happen to be there at the time, rather than pack your camera away put it in a plastic bag with a hole left open for the lens and try to capture the wetness and force of the most extreme rainfall you will probably ever experience. Outside the tropics, rainfall tends to appear weak and rather mistlike in photographs because it is not heavy enough to register on film, but the tropical monsoon provides a good opportunity to photograph a landscape bathed in drifting sheets of heavy rain.

Another seasonal type of bad weather comes from tropical cyclones which build up rapidly and can become very violent indeed. Once you find a sheltered place to take pictures from, try to capture the extraordinary effects of this extreme weather, such as palm trees bent almost double in the strong winds.

Tropical landscapes are as varied as any other, but one of the most well known is the rainforest, which for many people is the classic jungle, but is not easy to photograph well. Because it is so dense, there are few places where

Field workers *A high viewpoint enabled the photographer to include colourful figures working between the bushes*

you can see any distance, and most successful photographs of it are taken from beyond the margins of the forest itself—from across a river, or from a cliff top, a high rock or even from an aircraft. Nearer the forest, bright colours, such as those of tropical birds or flowers, can provide a sharp splash of colour as a contrast to the dark green vegetation.

A different type of tropical landscape, and probably the one with which most people are familiar, is that of the coast, whether coral reef, white sandy beach or mangrove swamp. One successful way of photographing a tropical beach is to use a telephoto lens to compress the planes of sea, beach and palm trees fringing the shore so that an almost abstract composition is formed from the distinctly different colours and textures of each area. Alternatively, a wide angle lens can include foreground details, such as exposed coral or shells washed up on the sand, together with a background seascape. Palm trees are frequently a part of tropical beach scenery, and are best photographed in a very graphic way, so that their shape dominates the picture. On the other hand,

Kilimanjaro *Like many volcanoes, it stands alone and its snowy summit contrasts with the foreground bush*

Sail silhouette *Dramatic skies are another feature of the tropics and can make subjects in their own right*

scape that can be revealed well in abstract compositions. The best pictures are usually taken within an hour or so of sunrise and sunset.

Mountain ranges close to the equator are quite different in appearance from those in higher latitudes. The most marked difference is that the heat of the tropical sun forces the snowline much higher. The vegetation changes noticeably as you climb up higher, with marked bands at various heights—a great variety of landscapes arranged vertically. In some parts of the tropics layer after layer of completely different landscapes can be seen on the slopes of a single mountain. This extraordinary sight makes a natural subject for photography. A long telephoto lens is essential and it is worth experimenting with different viewpoints until you can see a clear definition of each area in your composition.

Venezuelan cloud forest *By filling the frame with foliage hanging in the mist, a claustrophobic feel has been conveyed*

Thunder cloud *Unusual weather conditions often develop rapidly— do not leave your camera indoors!*

you can make use of them as effective silhouettes, particularly at sunset, as a frame for the distant sea and sky.

Palm trees are also a common feature in the cultivated landscapes of the tropics, either as closely packed lines of large plantations, or in small clumps dotted among rice fields. The highly distinctive appearance of such manmade landscapes makes them natural subjects for photography, particularly when the paddy fields are flooded in the wet season or under irrigation. At these times the waterlogged fields, delineated by narrow earth ridges, can make strong, graphic patterns. You can make the most of these in a creative way by choosing a high viewpoint and using a telephoto lens to catch the reflections of sky and clouds in the water.

In the early morning or late afternoon, if you photograph against the sun, you will obtain an effect of very high contrast, which can easily be made into abstract compositions. In some parts of tropical Asia, paddy rice is grown on spectacular terraces, whose lines follow the contours of the hill slopes. Again, the most effective views are generally those which look down on the descending fields, exploiting the patterns made by their ribbon-like structures.

A quite different type of tropical landscape is provided by the deserts. While deserts are by no means exclusively tropical, those in the tropics represent most people's ideas of what a desert should be. The sandy, dune landscapes can make spectacular pictures when photographed under low, raking sunlight which emphasizes the snaking relief of wind-forming drifts. The lack of vegetation in the driest deserts gives a starkness to the land-

Rural landscapes

All photographers, amateur and professional alike, tackle landscape photography at some point, but so many amateur efforts fail to make best use of the surroundings

When your holiday photographs are developed, do you ever wonder what happened to those glorious, sweeping views, those majestic, rolling landscapes? Did they really look so insignificant? Somehow, your memory and the picture do not agree.

Amateur landscape photographs are often disappointing. It is not the choice of subject that is usually at fault, but the conditions under which the subject was photographed. Professionals can wait for hours for a particular light, perhaps returning to the same spot day after day until they feel the conditions are perfect for the right picture. The amateur cannot usually afford such luxury and having found an attractive view snaps and moves on. But with careful forethought and an understanding of those elements which can really help to make your picture distinctive, you can avoid more disappointing photographs.

Light and weather are the landscape photographer's two most valuable and creative tools. A landscape can change dramatically when illuminated from different directions and it is well worth observing exactly how the look of the land alters as the sun moves in the sky.

Early morning and late evening are the times favoured most by landscape photographers. Shadows are softer then than in the middle of the day, and the warmer tones help to accentuate the form and texture of the land. Early morning light is particularly attractive when accompanied by a hazy, translucent mist. Think of a field full of sheep on a cold winter's morning. Nothing very remarkable to photograph, but the same scene photographed in a thick dawn mist could be an entirely different prospect. The sheep become ghostly figures, hardly discernible in the gloom, creating a haunting, more memorable image. Remember that you do not have to record factually every detail you see —your picture may have more impact if you hint at what is there instead.

The weather obviously has an influence on the quality of light. Bright, sunny days will cast more shadows, whatever time of day it is, while grey overcast days may tend to make your pictures rather flat and lacking in depth.

As a general rule, exaggerated weather conditions will probably produce the most dramatic shots. Some of the best landscape pictures have been taken in atrocious weather and even the most disappointing views can look considerably more exciting in a storm or in frosty weather. Use adverse conditions to show up the real bones of the country.

Learning to manipulate the light to improve your picture takes a good deal of experience. One of the most spectacular ways of using light in landscape is to shoot into the light itself. This may present some exposure problems, but by bracketing the exposure you should produce one image at least that approaches the effect you want. Look, too, for interesting shapes that would look effective in silhouette form and choose a vantage point that sets the subject against the light in the most original way.

Aerial view *This shot of a tractor tilling an American field makes very effective use of rural patterns. Its success lies in careful composition*

accentuate the dominance of a sky in a particularly flat region. A very high horizon, on the other hand, might be more appropriate if you wish to show the patterns of the land. As always, the only way to know what is best is to experiment with the viewfinder. Move it around, stand on a wall, crouch down low and see what is most suitable.

If the sky is rather bland, a polarizing filter will darken the sky tones without affecting the other colours. If shooting in black and white, a yellow, orange or red filter will increase the impact of a weak sky, darkening it to contrast dramatically with white clouds.

Stone boathouse *This lovely lakeside scene benefits from having a building included. It adds a point of interest and features some local stonework*

If you would like to do more landscape photography, but can never actually get started, it might be a good idea to set yourself a project. One idea is to choose a river and spend a day tracing its course, using it as a base from which to explore all the photographic possibilities as you go along. You might find a map useful, the kind that shows contours clearly, so you can work out where the best vantage points are likely to be. It is even worth considering spending a few days simply exploring a particular area to find the most suitable and attractive locations, spending time searching for the best viewpoint and thinking about the mood you wish to create.

The mood will largely depend on the kind of landscape you are going to photograph. It could be the traditional panoramic 'vista' type scene, the picture postcard variety, which embraces a wide area and can instantly give the viewer an impression of its beauty. Or it could be a smaller rural scene, depicting a part of farm life. You may prefer to close in on a subject, perhaps a group of animals grazing or an unusual pattern within the landscape.

It may be the beauty of the area you wish to capture, or the feel and style of an area, perhaps its characteristic boundary walls or unique farm buildings.

Composition in landscape is almost as important as lighting and weather. Knowing when things 'look right' is largely a question of experience, but a good way to develop your sense of composition is to study good landscape paintings, and see exactly why they work. The crucial balance is a complex combination of the right relationship between a number of elements like light and shade, different colours and proportion of foreground to sky. Try looking at a photograph that you instinctively feel does not look right and see if you can pinpoint the elements that seem to throw the picture off balance. Perhaps it is a tree that detracts too much from the main subject, diverting the eye

and causing confusion. If you can identify the particular aspect that is working against the balance, you are on the way to creating well composed photographs of your own.

One of the advantages of landscape photography is that its more static nature gives you more time to spend composing each shot carefully and choosing what appears within the frame. Before you press the shutter, train yourself to glance around the edges of the frame to make sure unwanted telephone lines or electricity pylons have not crept in and spoiled your picture.

One of the first decisions you will need to make regarding composition, particularly in the panorama type photograph, is where to put the horizon. The traditional choice is to have the sky take up two thirds of the picture, but this is by no means the rule. If the sky is particularly dramatic, a low horizon might enhance the picture. Similarly a low horizon will

Bare tree *A landscape does not have to include a wide view. It is equally effective to concentrate on a narrower area if it gives a feel of the region*

Terraced fields *The landscape varies widely throughout the world. If you travel abroad you should try to add a sense of place to your landscape*

just wandering around haphazardly, hoping for a few pictures.

Sometimes you may become engrossed in the composition and overall view of a subject that it is easy to gloss over the other interesting elements in the viewfinder. Seek out rich textures and interesting patterns that small portions of the whole scene can provide. Move in close to the textural surfaces of the soil, stone or rock formations as well as plant life itself. Look for patterns in light and shade, furrowed field, walls, the contours of land, colour relationships and the shapes of trees.

As far as equipment is concerned, there are no rules for the landscape photographer—most professionals working in this field have their own individual style and approach. You will almost certainly find that a tripod is useful, particularly in low light when you want to retain relatively small apertures and wide depth of field.

You can take an excellent range of photographs with a standard 50 mm lens, and if you have one, a medium telephoto around 105 or 135 mm to help you bring subjects closer and fill the frame. Longer focal length lenses tend to compress the distances between separate planes at distant viewpoints and you sacrifice depth, but of course you are able to magnify the subject. Some landscape photographers consistently work with lenses of around 300 mm, ideal for intricate patterns and rich textures.

When it comes to selecting film, you may decide that colour is the obvious choice. Certainly most professionals do work with colour transparencies but do not dismiss black and white too easily, as some really striking results can be achieved. When light is low, or if you want to achieve a particularly grainy effect, use a fast film.

All you can do now is start walking! The beauty is there—it is up to you to make the most of it.

Timber barns *A building does not have to be kept in the background. Sometimes it helps to compose a landscape so that buildings dominate the scene*

Grazing sheep *By combining these New Zealand mountains with a field of sheep this landscape has plenty of interest. The sky and the light also help the shot*

Another way to enhance your picture is to change your viewpoint and include a building somewhere in the picture. The eye will be drawn to it, as a point of interest, yet will take in the beauty of the scene too. It could be a single cottage, a hay barn, even a small cowshed, but its strategic placing within the overall composition can dramatically alter one's appreciation of the scene.

If your chosen theme is farmland, it should be easy to anticipate promising shots by learning about the farming calendar and talking to the farmer himself. Make it your business to find out when the lambing season begins, for instance, or when sheep shearing is to take place. Perhaps interesting new machinery is being delivered or installed. Get to know when ploughing, ditching, furrowing or planting takes place, work out your best vantage point and equipment needs before the event and make the most of the session. You will save a good deal of time and wasted effort and feel far more professional than

Chapter 5
Changing conditions
Fog, mist and haze

Reducing visibility and weakening both contrast and colours, fog, mist and haze seem at first glance to present enormous problems for the photographer. Yet there are a number of simple techniques to reduce their effect and there is no reason to feel restricted by this kind of weather. Indeed, with their distinctive lighting, fog, mist and haze can provide ideal conditions for certain shots.

Fog, mist and haze all serve to scatter the light from the sun, taking the edge off fine detail and dramatically reducing contrast. While for most photographs this is a disadvantage, the soft, diffuse lighting can often be more attractive than direct sunlight, particularly for close-ups. A conventional outdoor portrait is normally better without hard shadows, and a hazy sun can be an ideal light source. It gives definite, but soft, modelling to the face. Small landscape details, such as flowers, often benefit in the same way.

Because fog, mist and haze have greater effect over a distance, they all, to some extent, enhance the impression of depth in a scene. Backgrounds are

Early morning *By exposing for the bright sky, the photographer has used the mist to hide unwanted detail, and made an abstract pattern from the trees*

Blue bridge *In thick fog, your subject may be invisible until it is almost on top of you. The answer is to move in close and use a wide angle lens*

weaker, softer and brighter, and these conditions help foreground objects to stand out more clearly. This effect is known as *aerial perspective*, and can give a valuable sense of distance to a landscape. To take full advantage of aerial perspective, compose the image in such a way that distinct elements of the scene are visible at different distances from the camera—foreground detail, trees in the middle distance and distant hills on the horizon. A moderately wide-angle lens usually helps to reinforce this effect. Any subject that recedes from the camera, such as a road, benefits from this treatment.

On a hazy day, aerial perspective is quite gentle, but in mist and fog it becomes so pronounced that the landscape can appear to be made up of several distinct planes, stacked in front of each other. Apart from the graphic possibilities that this offers, it has two very practical uses in photography: it both isolates and conceals. By separating objects visually from their backgrounds, fog and mist provide clear, uncluttered outlines—individual trees, for example, can be isolated within a copse to provide a strong, simple image.

This is a positive use of fog—focusing attention on one subject—but it is also possible to use fog to hide backgrounds and settings that are either ugly or inappropriate. A line of pylons running across the hills in the distance, or the smoke stacks of a factory, may be an unavoidable part of the picture, particularly if you have only a limited choice of viewpoint. Here, a light mist will conveniently remove the intrusions from the image. In these ways, mist and fog can be thought of as very selective lighting conditions, so that if you are able to choose the time and day for a photograph, they actually give you some measure of control over your subject.

One of the most attractive features of fog and mist is that, being ground-level conditions, they sometimes appear as just a thin covering over the land, so that tall objects such as buildings and trees appear to rise out of a sea of white. On a foggy day, a high viewpoint can be very rewarding, particularly when the fog is clearing and wisps drift across the landscape. Subtle tonal gradations are possible under these conditions, when the thickness of the fog or mist changes across the scene.

Telephoto haze *By using a telephoto lens, you can exaggerate the effects of mist and use it to give a strong sense of depth to a picture*

Graininess is also enhanced by fog and mist, simply because they provide broad areas of continuous tone, and you can make a positive feature of this in the photograph. To exaggerate graininess, it is better to use black and white film. A high energy developer, particularly if you use it for push-processing, accentuates the grain even further, as does enlarging a small detail of the negative.

You can also emphasize grain when using colour film, though not as successfully as with black and white. Choose a 400 ASA (ISO) film—either negative or transparency—and confine the subject to the central portion of the frame. By enlarging the image more than usual the grain pattern becomes quite prominent.

If you use colour slide film, you can increase grain size in the same way as you can with black and white film—by push processing. Although this process is difficult it can be done at home, but most professional colour laboratories will do it for you, provided you ask for the service when you take the film in to be processed.

There are a number of other ways in which you can enhance the atmospheric effect of fog and mist. A telephoto lens makes the conditions seem more intense, while a wide-angle lens gives a better sense of aerial perspective. Haze, because it scatters blue and ultraviolet light most of all, can be enhanced on black and white film by using a blue filter, such as a Wratten 47. An effects filter, which softens the image to give an impression of mist, is sometimes useful, and a graduated mist filter can be used to affect only the distant part of the view, making it more realistic. To lower the contrast of a foggy picture even more, you could try overexposure and under-development.

Cutting through the mist

Despite the creative opportunities that fog, mist and haze offer, there are also many occasions when they are a nuisance. This is particularly true of haze—being less definite than the other two, it offers less scope for giving an unusual treatment to a picture. However, haze is more useful to a number of photographic techniques, principally because, unlike fog and mist, it scatters light selectively. The suspended particles in haze are so small that they scatter the shorter wavelengths—principally blue and ultraviolet—more than the rest. This is why a distant horizon often appears blue. Unfortunately, films are more sensitive than our eyes to blue and

Rocking chairs *Dense fog conceals ugly background detail, and you can use it to draw attention to the interesting shapes of objects close to the camera*

Mist on the water *Low lying mist soon disperses, so rise early. Choose a camera angle where the mist is lit from the side by the first rays of sun*

ultraviolet light, so that the effects of haze are more pronounced in a photograph than in the view itself.

Filters can do much to reduce the effect of haze. With black and white film, any filter that reduces blue gives some improvement, orange more than yellow, and red most of all. But the greatest

Cutting haze with infrared

One dramatically successful way of eliminating haze in a distant view is to use infrared film. This film is manufactured with an extra sensitivity to the invisible wavelengths beyond red—those that are least affected by scattering in the atmosphere. Infrared film is, however, also sensitive to other wavelengths, so that to get the best from it, you must use an appropriate filter. Black and white infrared film is sensitive to violet, blue and red, as well as to infrared, while colour Ektachrome infrared is sensitive to green, red and infrared—rather than blue, red and green, as in a normal colour film. Since it is the ultraviolet and blue end of the spectrum that contributes most to the effects of haze, a yellow or orange filter, at the very least, is essential.

Colour infrared film has, in addition to its haze-clearing properties, the more startling effect of false colour, particularly with living vegetation, which it records as red or magenta instead of green. Black and white infrared film, on the other hand,

can be used as a more normal substitute for regular film: with a red filter such as a Wratten 25 or 29, some of the visible spectrum contributes to the picture, but with an 87 filter, which is visually opaque, the haze penetration and the contrast are intense. In both cases, vegetation appears very bright, because the green chlorophyll in plants reflects infrared light very strongly. For exposure, follow the instructions packed in the film, bearing in mind that your exposure meter is not sensitive to infrared. An example of haze penetration with IR film is shown on page 106.

Most lenses are designed to focus only visible light, and with infrared film you must focus a little nearer than you would normally. Most lens mounts are marked with a red dot next to the focusing index— use this as your new focusing mark.

While infrared film is ideal for eliminating haze, it actually gives worse results than normal film in fog; the water droplets are so large that they reflect all wavelengths, especially infrared.

Infrared cityscape *Dust particles which scatter light and cause haze have no effect on infrared. But by using a special film and a filter which blocks all wavelengths except IR, haze can be virtually eliminated. The lower picture was taken on conventional film*

effect is given by a Wratten 29 deep red filter. Unfortunately, with such a darkly coloured filter in place exposure must be increased by four stops.

With colour film, really effective haze penetration is not possible because strong coloured filters cannot be used. An ultraviolet filter helps a little, but its effect is only really obvious at high altitudes, where ultraviolet scattering is strongest. Some ultraviolet filters have a pale yellow tinge to counter the blue scattering visible when a telephoto lens is used for a distant view. However, when using a telephoto, the simplest way to control haze is to carefully choose the time of day and the viewpoint. Generally, haze is weakest early in the morning and strongest in the early afternoon. It is also most obvious with backlighting. If you have the choice, select a camera position where the sun is behind or to one side of you.

Depending on the camera position, you may find that the most effective filter is a polarizer. Although better known for its more obvious properties of darkening blue skies and cutting reflections from non-metallic surfaces, one of the most useful functions of polarizing filters is to eliminate reflections from haze particles—at least, those at right angles to the direction of the sun —and to improve contrast and colour saturation. Contrast can also be improved by using an effective lens hood.

With both black and white and colour film, you can heighten contrast further by increasing the development, but this increases graininess. If you are prepared to accept the extra graininess, the slight increase in contrast may be valuable.

Nevertheless, the most certain way of avoiding the effects of haze is to move close to your subject. The nearer you are, the less atmosphere and so the fewer particles there are in front of the camera. This means, where possible, using a wide angle lens. Also, because subtle and neutral hues make it easy for the eye to distinguish the bluish cast that is characteristic of haze, a brightly coloured subject is better.

Exposure control

Because of the light scattering effect, fog and mist can often present problems with exposure. Fog and mist generally bring an overall bright tone to a scene, so that if you follow your meter's reading unswervingly, you run the risk of an underexposed photograph. Exposure meters average the light that falls on their cells from different parts of the subject, and deliver a setting that produces a mid-toned image. If most of the picture area is taken up with white mist, the exposure that your meter recom-

mends results in an image that is grey rather than white. The solution is to decide how much lighter than average you want a foggy scene to appear, and increase the exposure accordingly. The exact amount depends on the particular situation, but generally an extra one or one and a half stops gives good results. However, if you want to capture the gloom of a misty day, follow the meter reading. If, as an experiment, you take a range of bracketed exposures of a fog-bound view, you should find that several look acceptable—what alters is the mood of the picture.

Because fog and mist tend to produce soft, muted colours, any colour cast is immediately obvious. The colour temperature of light on a foggy day is high— about 7500K—and unless some correction filtration is applied, this results in a pale blue cast. Some films produce a heavier cast than others, and all the Ektachrome emulsions look particularly cool in overcast or misty weather. The solution is to use an 81 series filter—an 81A, 81B or 81C—all of which warm up the picture and eliminate any blue cast.

Finally, it is important to look after your equipment carefully in fog and mist. The air in these conditions is heavily saturated with water, and condensation is often a problem particularly if your camera is cold. Use a soft dry cloth and lens tissues to remove droplets as soon as they form, not only from the surface of the lens, where they will spoil the image, but from the entire body; if not, water may penetrate the mechanisms. Waterpoofing the camera in a plastic bag is usually unnecessary, but it is important to keep your camera in a shoulder bag except when you are actually taking a shot.

Learning to exercise some photographic control over weather conditions such as these, either by accentuating their most useful characteristics or suppressing those that you do not want, extends the range of conditions under which you can successfully take good photographs. This in turn gives you the opportunity to explore landscapes and other outdoor subjects in a variety of ways, rather than just in stereotyped 'good weather'.

Rain

Do not be discouraged by the prospect of a rainy day. Take your camera out and discover the potential of marvellous images in wet conditions

The most interesting photographs are not necessarily those which are taken in bright sunshine. Unfortunately, most photographers regard the first few drops of rain as a signal for them to take to the darkroom, or even to forget about photography altogether. This is a pity, since a rainy day is actually a very good time to achieve those subtle and occasionally dramatic effects which are just not possible when the sun is shining over your left shoulder, in the accepted fashion. Once you decide to brave the rain, with waterproof boots, a raincoat and some protection for your camera, you will find that many creative possibilities for photography exist.

Everyone has a different image of rain in their mind's eye. Quite often these images will be very evocative of a mood, a place or a way of life. It is a challenge to capture such images on film, and to recreate the very feeling of rain for whoever views the picture. Rain can vary from soft, permeating drizzle to the streaming torrents of a monsoon, so there is a wide variety of possible images.

Rain itself can be hard to photograph. Our visual impression of rain includes its movement, and even though we do not see individual drops, we can perceive it falling even when it is such fine drizzle that the familar streak effect is not apparent. A photograph taken under such conditions would show nothing of the rain, and even what the eye sees as obvious rain may not register on a photograph as anything more than a general mistiness.

Heavier rain, however, will show up in a photograph as streaked lines, though the exact image will depend on the focus point and the depth of field. With a restricted depth of field, the streak effect may be less apparent than when a wide range is in focus.

We usually look towards a dark object to establish how heavily the rain is falling, and the same is true if you want to portray the rain in a photograph. The most realistic impression is often gained by showing the rain as short streaks, but this effect requires a surprisingly fast shutter speed, generally difficult to give because of the dimness of the light. And unless it is raining very hard, you may find when you see the picture that there were very few raindrops close enough to the camera, or within its depth of field, to register in this way.

Using electronic flash, either at night or as fill-in, it is possible to isolate individual raindrops as they fall. But this may give an effect quite unlike rain. The few drops that are close enough to the camera to be seen clearly may be overexposed, while farther away the drops merge into a general mistiness.

Pictures which feature the rain itself are probably most effective where there is an additional subject fairly close to the

Rosebud *Leaves and flowers look fresh and sparkling after rain, when tiny beads of water cling to their surfaces, and it is well worth taking close-ups*

camera on which you are focusing. Then you will be restricting the depth of field to the general vicinity of your subject, and the rain itself will be apparent to the camera. Typical subjects include people forced to stand in the rain, or just sheltering from the rain in a doorway or under a street market stall's awning.

In general, you may find it more rewarding to picture the effects of rain rather than the rain itself.

One of the most attractive qualities of a rainy day is the transformation that occurs when everything becomes wet. Even the most mundane surfaces, such as the pavements, become shimmering, glistening pools of reflected light. The many different types of reflections created by the water are subjects in themselves and you could spend your rainy day absorbed in photographing these. Look, in particular for buildings, cars, or street lamps reflected in the surface of a pavement. Rough surfaces, such as a cobbled street, where the water gathers unevenly, create interesting broken up, impressionistic reflections. Normally still water, spattered with raindrops, will have almost the same effect. If you focus just on the surface of the water, the possibilities of playing with the reflections presented to you in a creative way are practically endless if you think carefully.

Such conditions often occur in showery weather. The sort of pictures you take will often depend on the nature of the rain, and showery weather in particular provides many opportunities for photography. There is always the chance of a sudden downpour which will create considerable panic in the streets. People run for cover, struggle with umbrellas and rainhats, gutters overflow into temporary waterfalls, and cats retreat disdainfully to the nearest doorway, while children seem to be the only ones to react with excitement and exuberance. Toddlers, in particular, and regard-

Open air concert *A rainy day is a good time for candid pictures, and may produce some amusing images*

Window *A normally dull view may appear to be much more attractive when seen through a screen of pearly raindrops*

less of their footwear, usually rush gleefully to jump in the nearest puddle. See how the spectators at a sporting event cope with an unexpected shower as colourful umbrellas and makeshift headpieces appear as if by magic. Generally, people are so preoccupied with preserving their dignity on these occasions that they fail to notice what amusing subjects they make for the candid camera.

Awnings and trees have their own ready-made source of pictures in rain—they usually have a good supply of unexpected large drips to catch out the unwary passer by. Wait patiently and unobtrusively to catch the expression of disgust as someone receives a drip down the back of their neck.

As you become aware of the rain as a subject for photography, you will notice that there are actually many different types of rain. A very thin drizzle can be entered bravely, with your camera protected by a plastic bag. This type of rain acts as a soft screen between you and your subject, and the effect is roughly simiiar to that given by a soft focus filter. On the other hand, a heavy monsoon-like downpour may be too much for the plastic bag, and it is best to photograph from some sort of shelter.

A rainy day often requires fast film, since the light level will be very low in a real downpour, but do not try to give too much exposure or you will destroy the

Rickshaw *Very heavy rain can be shown as streaks with a fast shutter speed, but is best photographed from shelter*

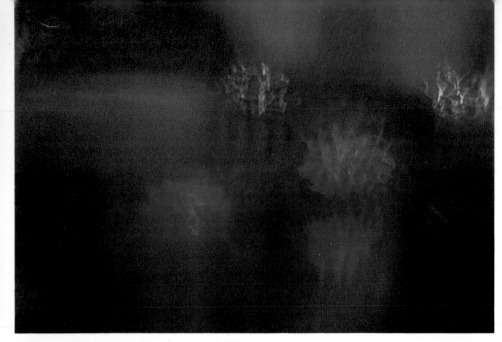

pictures can be achieved by concentrating on details and close-ups such as these. Note how the colours of flowers or leaves, for example, change when they become wet. See that, in close-up, the individual droplets distort the surface of the subject beneath, and act as miniature magnifying glasses. Look out for the reflective quality of the water, which in strong light brings myriad highlights in to play.

Another effect often seen after rain has just passed is the rainbow. These

Lights *Night lights in the rain, photographed through a window, form blurred, abstract images*

Sky *A dramatic skyscape often precedes a cloudburst, and in open country it is revealed at its best*

heavy mood which accompanies such rain. Fast film has the drawback of giving less vivid colours and lower contrast, which may result in disappointing pictures. Look for brightly coloured objects as a contrast, such as yellow mackintoshes, red traffic lights or bright green leaves. When the rain is falling fairly fast, people automatically put their lights on to compensate for the lost daylight, whether car lights or domestic lamps. You can use these to great effect in your photographs.

A rain storm is not the best place for a camera, and although a few drops of rain on the casing or lens filter will do no harm, you will probably prefer to carry out your rain photography from shelter. Raindrops on a window are a classic subject, either in their own right as a close-up, or as part of a picture with

someone looking out at the rain.

The few minutes after heavy rain has stopped are frequently a rewarding time for photography. This is the moment when you sometimes see a shaft of sunlight breaking through the tail end of the storm clouds, and when the possibilities of extraordinary backlighting effects must be grasped before the combination of wind and sun dries everything out. Droplets of rain hanging on to branches, leaves, flowers and spiders' webs, for example, make attractive photographs, particularly when backlit so that the water glistens on the subject.

With these smaller subjects, it is worth taking a close-up shot, throwing the background out of focus, so that the maximum attention is given to the effect of the water. Some of the most exciting

occur when a fairly low sun shines on rain, and are visible opposite the sun in the sky. They are most effective when seen against dark clouds.

Rainbows often last a short time only, so it is not possible to select your viewpoint at leisure. But by knowing the circumstances in which they appear, you can be on the alert and watching for a good opportunity to take the picture. A wide angle lens will help to show the curvature and any inner or outer bows, while a telephoto can be useful for concentrating on the place where the rainbow is seen against ground features, lending them eerie colours. You can give a normal meter exposure when photographing a rainbow, though half a stop of underexposure may heighten the dramatic effect and emphasize the colours dramatically.

Wet crowd *The two figures in raincoats (below) provide a centre of interest among the sea of umbrellas—they not only stand out but lead the eye in to the picture*

Solo leaf *Water drops add an atmospheric element, reminiscent of foggy autumn mornings. Such details can easily be set up by the photographer. An interesting background is also important to provide a setting for the subject*

Umbrella *Even the dullest rainy day provides opportunities for amusing, almost abstract, candid shots like this man beneath an umbrella (right)*

Rain *With a long exposure, moving coloured objects and lights become more or less blurred streaks—particularly effective against the blacks of night*

Shower *The selective view of a long telephoto was exploited here to isolate the figures standing in the rain*

Sun and flowers *Octagonal flare spots need not spoil your picture. In this image they echo the drops on the leaves*

Sunrise and sunset

Sunrises and sunsets can make many otherwise mundane scenes look spectacular, but you need imagination to create an eyecatching image and restraint to avoid the cliché

Few photographers can resist the attraction of sunsets and sunrises. With their brilliant glowing colours and dramatic lighting, they are instantly photogenic, and, with the right exposure, invariably give an attractive picture. Yet many sunset pictures are pleasant rather than outstanding and to take a really stunning sunset, you must do more than merely point the camera at the sinking sun and press the shutter.

While beautiful sunsets are common enough in many parts of the world, really spectacular skies are comparatively rare—it needs a particular combination of atmospheric conditions to give the classic image of a fiery disc sinking slowly in a copper sky amidst clouds ablaze with purple and gold.

At rising and setting, the sun is naturally a warmer colour than at other times of day because, at a low angle, its rays have to travel further through the atmosphere. But for a really red sunset, there needs to be some impurities in the atmosphere to help scatter the blue light—sunsets are rarely very red in clear weather. The best sunsets tend to occur not after a hot, still day, but when the weather suddenly clears after a change-

able day. If this type of weather is forecast, it is worth looking for a suitable vantage point.

When the atmosphere is polluted, though, the sunset may be very red even in clear weather—tropical sunsets are often very red because of the dust in the atmosphere.

Some of the most spectacular sunsets in the northern hemisphere were seen after the eruption of Mount Saint Helens in 1979 filled the atmosphere with volcanic dust which spread westwards from the volcano. On a more mundane level, urban pollution, while generally undesirable, does help to produce some attractive sunsets and sunrises. If you live near a heavy industrial area, it is worth getting up early to catch the sun rising red behind the gaunt silhouettes of the factories.

Nevertheless, for the greatest spectacle clouds are important, preferably close to the horizon, in different formations and at different heights. Clouds reflect and absorb the light, and the most interesting sunsets occur when there is a wide variety of clouds at the same time. In unsettled weather, thick woolly cumulus often looks effective, particularly

when combined with higher, thin layers. Tropical sunsets appear so marvellous because the towering thunderheads of cloud that have built up during the afternoon heat are usually broken up after a short, heavy storm and by sunset these allow an intricate play of light to filter through. However, there is always the chance that the sun may sink behind a cloud bank before it reaches the horizon and not reappear before it sets. A sun heavily dimmed by cloud can actually appear more colourful on film than in reality, as the grey clouds often reproduce as blue or purple on film. Take the time to select a few of the best features of any particular sunset and concentrate on these. Choose the camera technique that will focus attention on these features.

For instance, under certain conditions, the disc of the sun itself may be an interesting subject. In hazy weather, as with the tropical sunset, the disc appears to be enlarged and slightly patterned, and if the haze becomes thicker towards the horizon, the red sun may seem to set in mid air. In this case, use a telephoto lens to emphasize the effect.

You can also focus on the surrounding sky, taking either a general view that includes the sun, or a detail of the cloud formation, underlit, backlit or streaked with colour. You can create dramatic or unusual effects by emphasizing different areas of balance within the frame, for instance, darker colours on top, making the picture seem top heavy. If you isolate a small area of sky, you can obtain many interesting variations by using the lines and colours to create an abstract pattern.

Sunrise in south Australia *Try using the colourful light of the low sun as a backlight to create strong foreground silhouettes*

Lake Diebo, Mali *A wide angle lens allows you to take in a wider scene for added interest and produces more than just a 'sunrise'*

Alternatively, you may want to treat sunrise or sunset as part of a landscape. In this case, the horizon, and therefore the viewpoint, becomes a major consideration. Contrast is always high at these times of day, and the successful balance of contrast levels with subject matter is a delicate task. Details in the foreground are necessarily backlit, and become silhouetted against the sky. The brighter and less cloudy a sunset or sunrise, the more pronounced the silhouette will be.

Silhouettes are a very useful graphic technique when you are concentrating on the actual disc of the sun, which will benefit considerably from a positive shape juxtaposed in the foreground, but without a colour to compete with the sunset itself.

At sunset or sunrise, it is usually worth choosing foreground details with interesting outlines. Set the exposure according to the effect you want. An average exposure may show some foreground detail, but will usually give weaker colours to the sky itself. An exposure based on the ligher areas of the sky will give deep, saturated colours and an intense silhouette. It is a mistake, however, to expose for the foreground as the brilliant sky colours will almost certainly be washed out. A graduated neutral filter can help to show both the sunset and the foreground however.

Foregrounds often pose a problem with sunset shots, particularly if the sky is not very interesting. Unless there is a fascinating silhouette, it is important to include some detail in the foreground to enliven the picture. The area immediately in front of the camera should therefore be fairly light in colour, otherwise it may be impossible to achieve the correct exposure—ideally it should be light enough to balance the sky. A large expanse of water—the sea, for instance—that catches the reflection of the sky, and adds subtle changes, is ideal. Mud flats or beaches serve a similar purpose, particularly when rounded off with a small silhouetted figure or boat.

Twilight offers very different possibilities. Just occasionally, when the weather conditions are right, there may be a vivid afterglow, when the sun, no longer visible, lights up very high clouds in a spectacular way for a moment

Malaysian fishermen *Brilliant colours are not essential for a dawn scene*
Death valley *In the opposite direction to a sunset, you may find a patch of warm colour as the last rays of light stretch across the landscape.*
Pastoral scene *Instead of concentrating on the sky, the photographer has exposed this shot to feature the pastoral scene in the foreground.* **Waves** *Rather than including the sky itself, this shot combines its reflection with the water*

or so. For its rarity, this effect is nearly always worth photographing.

Twilight is also useful photographically because it tends to create an even-toned area of sky that graduates smoothly into darkness above. This can produce an uncluttered background for silhouettes, and give a large, clear reflection in water, which can help rivers and lakes to stand out clearly in a distant landscape view.

Twilight produces soft pastel colours, and the long exposures which are necessary at this light level tend to make colours intermingle and produce dramatic swirling effects. A particular feature of shooting pictures in the early morning and evening is the peculiar, almost uneasy sense of quietness that exists at these times. Try to capture this feeling in your photographs. The illumination is invariably very blue in colour, even when there is a rosy glow in the direction of the sun. Bear this in mind, as the

results may otherwise surprise you.

In photographs, sunsets and sunrises are difficult to tell apart. They are quite different events to see but a still shot cannot normally distinguish between them—except, perhaps, in cities where pollution in the atmosphere at different times of day causes a particular effect with which you are familiar.

Nevertheless, local weather conditions may make a difference at any one place. For example, in many mountainous areas, dawn finds the valleys filled with cloud, from which the peaks stand clear. By late afternoon these peaks may be shrouded. If you are planning to take sunset or sunrise photographs in an unfamiliar place, it may be a good idea to check these conditions.

Because there are fewer people around, it may be easier taking pictures at sunrise, particularly if you are taking a landscape picture of a well known beauty spot, but in general, sunrises are

more difficult to plan for. You may have to decide the location on the previous day, since you will then have to set up the camera in semi-darkness. Predicting the exact point where the sun breaks the horizon is easy only in the tropics, where the sun rises almost vertically in much the same place every-day. Everywhere else the sun rises at an angle, so that the first glow you see is not where the sun will eventually rise. So if you are planning a shot so that the sun clears the horizon at a precise point, you may have to do a dry run the day before.

Both at sunrise and sunset, however, the light changes very quickly, and your reactions must be sharp to take advantage of this rapid change. One way to record these effects is to shoot a sequence of photographs several minutes apart as the sun is setting or rising. This will enable you to inspect every small detail and decide the best time to shoot for the best picture.

Sunlit building *Direct light can make your shots attractive, but it is equally effective to use the light as it is reflected from other subjects*

Arizona rocks *Warm light reflected in the rocks creates an attractive sunset shot—without the sun itself. The dark foreground shapes add extra effect*

Dawn at 2000 metres *The graduated intensity of the blue sky and the dark, solid foreground create an attractive sunrise without dramatic colours*

Yachts in mist *This shot does not exploit the light usually associated with a sunrise, but gains atmosphere from the diffused, golden light caused by the mist*

Sun and pylon *For silhouette shots it is worth thinking of more unusual subjects to place in the foreground. A 300 mm lens is ideal for this purpose*

Landscape *For some shots, a low sun can be used to give extra qualities to a scene which already has enough interest to make an attractive photograph*

Snow

Snow transforms landscapes and cityscapes, provides endless subjects for close-ups and gives an excellent opportunity for portrait and action shots, as long as you take a little more care with exposures

Snow is undoubtedly one of the most beautiful phenomena in nature. However, because it is so beautiful it is all too easy just to reach for the camera and shoot pictures almost blindly, assuming that an attractive scene will automatically make an attractive and creative picture. In fact, the blanket of whiteness that envelops everything familiar often looks less good on film than it seemed at the time. Very often the whiteness is either overpowering or simply monotonous in a photograph. Some shots may well be overexposed, while others are grey and dull. But the problems that snow poses for the photographer, whether technical or aesthetic, can be overcome by intelligent handling of contrast and colour.

For the photographer, the overall whiteness is the most striking feature of any snowy scene and tends to dictate the approach, both technically and creatively, whether you are taking landscapes, portraits or abstracts. One point particularly worth remembering—it is usually necessary to find something which contrasts in colour or tone with the snow in order to achieve a successful and attractive image.

If you are taking a landscape, a bright subject in the foreground—perhaps some winter berries on a tree, a car, a person in colourful winter clothing or simply a child's woollen mitten mislaid in the rush to go tobogganing—can be useful in your composition, not only to add colour, but to give an idea of scale. Once the snow has enveloped everything in a white blanket, it is very easy to lose the sense of scale in a photograph, without some reference to a familiar object.

On the other hand, you can use the extreme whiteness to create surreal, high key effects. This is often easier using black and white film, where it is possible to increase the contrast in the printing stage. A row of trees can become jet black skeletons on a pure white background, for example. You can create very simple, graphic images which set out to make the viewer shiver just to look at them. The essence of the technique is to reduce everything to its basics, and convey the starkness of a winter country landscape.

Drawing on this experience, you can try to create the same sort of effects in colour. In general the only way to control contrast in colour is by choosing your film to start with. Slow films have high contrast, and fast films lower contrast. Snow scenes taken on fast colour film can become very pale and washed out. On high contrast film, however, you can record and even emphasize the wide range of brightnesses in a snowy scene.

Many of the details of the texture of snow are low in contrast, and high contrast film is useful for emphasizing these. On the other hand, under some circumstances the opposite approach might be more suitable, particularly in the city, where it might be more difficult to keep your images simple enough for the high contrast approach. You may, for example, need to include both the snow and details in stonework or buildings, in which case a faster, lower contrast film may give a more pleasing result.

The quality of light can be quite unlike

Sun and snow *Shooting into the sun can create sparkling, surreal images— particularly if you do not compensate for the bright sun when exposing*

Shadows *Even simple objects such as sticks can produce unusual shadow patterns, which appear pale blue when the sky is clear*

Garden steps *Simple subjects with geometrical shapes work well when snow covered so that their lines and shapes are clearly outlined. A low sun provides an ideal light for revealing the texture of the snow.*
Red railings *Bright colours, reds in particular, contrast well with the cold whiteness of snow because of their warmth. In this picture, a close-up of snow and railing spikes makes an abstract design of red and white, while the grey background is thrown out of focus to concentrate attention on the design.* **Tree and landscape** *Late afternoon sunshine often brings a warm, rosy glow to a snowscape which is worth waiting for. If you are shooting into the sun at this time, look for subjects silhouetted against the pale sky beyond.*
Snowman *Pictures of snowmen often fail because the subject does not stand out against a predominantly white background. As this picture shows, however, a carefully chosen viewpoint makes all the difference, contrasting the snowman against some darker trees behind.* **City streets** *Snow in towns and cities need not always look like a dreary, grey slush. If you take pictures at night, you will find that snow contrasts well with the differently coloured lights. Taken on Ektachrome 200 using a tripod to steady the 100 mm lens*

any other when the weather is snowy. It is a good idea to make the most of this light, since it is as much a feature of a snowy landscape as the snow itself. The white covering reflects light upwards, reversing the normal situation where the light comes from above. When the sky is overcast, the lighting is as flat as it can ever be, and there is an almost complete lack of directionality involved. People's faces glow, and their wrinkles disappear. Even indoors, the lighting becomes strange—ceilings reflect the snow and a person's face at a window reveals that there is snow on the ground, even if the picture does not show it.

The colour of the light, even on an overcast day, can vary enormously. If the sky is quite bright, at midday, film can reproduce colours very faithfully, and the subtle background grey can add to the feel of the shot without recourse to filters. But as the cloud cover thickens and the sky gets darker, the overall colour can rapidly turn blue, requiring an 81 series filter unless you feel that the blue colour will add to the mood.

On a sunny day, everything seems brilliant, and the light reflected from the ground adds to the general illumination. Although the snow appears white, all the shadows are blue since they are illuminated solely by the blue sky. Under these conditions, oddly enough, an 81 series filter can produce a more pleasing colour rendering by removing some of the blue content.

There is some debate about the correct exposure to give in snowy conditions. As always, exposure for transparency film is far more critical, so this is one occasion where negative film can give better results. The problem is that a meter is likely to give an exposure which will render the scene as an overall grey, so there is a tendency to underexpose. This seems to be more of a problem on overcast days than on sunny days, but it is responsible for the failure of many snow pictures. To make matters worse, any overexposure results in unrelieved expanses of white with no tones whatsoever. While half a stop overexposure is probably the best compromise, there are cases where normal exposure, or even half a stop of underexposure, can produce a better picture. To be on the safe side, take a reading from a standard grey card for a mid reading. If you bracket, give a range of half stop intervals between half a stop under to one stop over the meter reading to ensure good exposure.

A bright blue sky is a useful source of colour in a snow picture. If the sky is milky rather than deep blue, a polarizing filter may help, but when the sky is really clear, as it can be at ski resorts, a polarizing filter can easily turn parts of the sky almost totally black.

You can, however, use snow to create unusual pictures by the simple technique of underexposing and shooting against the light. This can give the appearance of moonlight glinting on rooftops, for example. Long exposures taken in ths way can produce strangely coloured results as colours shift slightly, and the effects of lens flare can also produce interesting results.

Pictures taken against the sun can often show the texture of the snow itself, with small crystals sparkling. Keep an eye open for shadows of trees seen against the sun—with a wide angle lens in particular these can stand out very dramatically.

Drifts of snow can be worth studying in their own right. They offer great potential for abstract shots, if you close in and remove all other reference points. Concentrate on the shadows and the texture of the snow. By choosing your viewpoint you may be able to turn a fairly small drift into what seems to be a huge mountain.

When snow is on the ground, you may have the chance to take extraordinary night shots. Snow can reflect a large amount of light and even a streetlight can provide enough illumination for an interesting picture, although you may need a tripod at this stage to achieve a sharp picture. If it is a clear night, you may be able to shoot scenes lit only by moonlight. In this case look for the places where the snow is undisturbed and where it will glisten in the moonlight. If you have access to a fairly high viewpoint, you will be able to photograph the rooftops in your town or village in such a way that the different angles and shapes make an abstract composition.

In a city at night during snowy weather, the differently coloured light sources can give you enough subjects for a whole series of photographs. Lights from cafés and shops contrast well with the whiteness of the snow, while the coloured tail lights of cars can provide splashes of warm red against either a frozen white or a slushy grey road. And if you are in the city, where there are cars parked, look out for that strange effect which occurs when a car has been parked before it started snowing, then has moved away, leaving a clear patch on the ground to contrast with the white snow.

Although in most large towns and cities the snow may be cleared away, or

Landscape *Bare trees and hedges in snow are a classic theme. A telephoto shot emphasizes the patterns made by the field boundaries*

Chalets *The most interesting details in a landscape can be isolated with a telephoto lens so as not to include any other distracting elements*

Snowball fight *A fast shutter speed freezes the action of both people and snowballs which show up best against a dark, clear background*

bright flakes may result in the flash underexposing the rest of the scene.

If the temperature is well below freezing, you may be able to photograph individual snow crystals. They will melt rapidly unless you prepare a cold surface for them. Leave some dark material outdoors, protected from the snow, so that it reaches the outside temperature, then any flakes which fall on it will not melt, and you can photograph them, under cover outdoors, at your leisure. Your main problem will be preventing your breath from melting them, so use a telephoto lens with extension tubes or bellows to get a reasonably large image without having to move too close.

Another area to explore during a fall of snow is that of human interest. Most people enjoy the snow enormously and there is something about it which tends to make people uninhibited about their enjoyment. It is a particularly rewarding time for portraits, candid and action shots as children build snowmen and have snowball fights and people try to skate on frozen ponds and toboggan down slopes. Usually, the clothing people choose at this time is warm and colourful, and if not, faces themselves can be rosy enough to act as a point of colour in an otherwise white scene.

may simply melt more quickly because of the slightly higher temperature, in the countryside the snow may persist far longer. If it does, it may be worth making an expedition to find untouched carpets of snow, trees laden with snow, animal tracks, and scenes which you photographed in the summer, totally transformed. You could take along some of your earlier shots to help you capture the same scene. Bear in mind that the roads are likely to be treacherous.

When snow is actually falling, exposure times shorter than 1/250 second should capture snowflakes in the air. A long exposure, around 1/30 second, shows them as hazy streaks, which can give a scene a romantic appearance. A flash exposure as snow is falling shows the nearer flakes very bright and blurred, though frozen in motion, and emphasizes the snowfall. It would be better to use a manual exposure setting rather than an automatic one, as the

Chapter 6
Photographing buildings
Your neighbourhood

One of the greatest challenges for any photographer is to find interesting pictures in that most familiar of areas—your own neighbourhood. On holiday in faraway places, every back street, every wall, every roof seems interesting and worth photographing. The street where you live or work, on the other hand, may seem comparatively dull.

Someone visiting your area from another part of the world, however, might find your neighbourhood fascinating, just as you find theirs. The difficulty lies in looking at your area with fresh eyes. There are very good reasons for doing so. The challenge will teach you more about photography, which will stand you in good stead when confronted with the unfamiliar. The pictures should reveal something about your area which you should be able to see better than an outsider.

One way of looking at your area with fresh eyes is to set yourself a professional style assignment, with a specific objective. Imagine that you have been asked to capture the spirit and appearance of the area for a colour supplement article, or to show people living on the other side of the world what life in your

From a window *Even a window view has potential. Here, the photographer chose a moment when the winter light invested the scene with atmosphere*

Locals *Your neighbours should also be considered as likely subjects—they will be familiar with you and so relaxed in front of your camera*

surrounding area is really like.

A professional faced with this assignment would spend a considerable time simply looking around, trying to get the feel of the place and noticing the age and types of buildings, assessing the people that live and work there, and choosing either typical or interesting examples. In some ways you have a head start, since you already know so much about the area and its population.

For example, unless you live on a

housing estate which was all built at the same time, it is quite likely that you will find buildings of different ages mixed together. You may not even previously have noticed that some buildings are considerably older than the rest and have survived later rebuilding programmes. Look for telltale signs such as the design of doors, windows and roofs as well as the obvious construction material. These features are ones that change most rapidly.

Even if you do live on an estate where all the houses are similar, small fittings and little quirks of design will make your estate different from those elsewhere, so look closely. If together they do not inspire you to make a photograph out of them, close in on them until they do. If the light is wrong, come back another day when it is. In your own neighbourhood you can do this easily. A plain brick wall can look good close up when the light is coming from the side. If there is a

West Coast suburbia *Photographer Bill Owen has been documenting his home area in Dublin, California, for years. These two contrasting views show the difference between a distant and an involved approach. The aerial shot shows a view which is seldom seen, and emphasizes the design of the roads and the repetitive, uniform pattern of the houses. Such features are less obvious at close range. But this gives a fuller idea of the way people live*

patch of moss or a smear of paint on it, so much the better—make these the ingredients of a colourful abstract that will still be recognizable. But while such details can often provide the most rewarding subjects for photography, do not forget to show the overall scene as well, or there will be no structure to your series of pictures—they will be merely a collection of apparently unrelated shots.

Look for peculiarities and differences. Try and remember what struck you when you first saw the area, and you may be able to transform the mundane into the interesting. Such details as the electricity and telephone wiring can often make all the difference to an area. In many places the sky at roof level is festooned with cables for these services, while elsewhere they run underground with the occasional box somewhere in the street for access. Even these are essential features of the area, which you only notice when they are changed. Street lamps, too, tend to be characteristic of an area, and the glass envelopes of the lamps can be intriguing when seen

through a telephoto lens.

The very roadways and pavements can be worth photographing, particularly in older areas. Such mundane features as manhole covers frequently have complex patterns, and some people have made a study of the different variations that can occur in even a small area.

Photographs are often more impressive when presented as a complete series rather than as individual images. Your own neighbourhood may be an ideal place to build up such a series—not only are you more likely to be able to find the time to go out and take a few shots when the conditions are just right, but also your familiarity with the locality will enable you to notice details more readily. Windows, shopfronts, doors or door handles, gardens or abstracts are the sort of subjects which can offer enough scope to build up a series in a limited area.

A photoessay which gives a general view is easy if you live in a small neighbourhood, such as a village or small town, but if you live in a city you may find that the best approach is to decide to

study just one particular aspect of the place. For instance, you can make an interesting essay on the area by exploring the people and the way in which they live.

There are many aspects of the people of a neighbourhood that are worth concentrating on. There are, for example that group of people usually described as 'characters'. To be fair, everyone has a character of their own, but some express their character more visibly than others and are better subjects for photography. One usually thinks of 'characters' as being elderly, but the young enthusiast cleaning his car, as he always does on Saturday mornings, or the harrassed housewife with three children in tow, both form part of the everyday scene and may be typical of the local population. A modern housing estate will have a high proportion of young people, while more sedate areas tend to have many retired people in them. Concentrate on these differences to reveal the character of the area.

Even over a matter of a few years the people change. Old people die, some

It is worth remembering that a great deal of the interest in old photographs lies in the fashions that were current at the time. But consider how much more rapidly fashions and crazes change today. This is most noticeable with young people—even a year later their fashions seem quaint and amusing—but older people change as well. Crazes, too, will suddenly appear on the streets and will then die away. Some will be peculiar to your area so they will be well worth photographing as part of the changing scene of the neighbourhood.

In large cities, in particular, you will often find small communities of immigrants who have settled together and built up their own area in a very distinctive style. Whether they are expatriate British in India or Chinese immigrants in Los Angeles you will find that they have their own shops and cafés, clubs and churches. By concentrating on a small neighbourhood like this and returning to photograph it over several weeks, you may get to know your way around and make friends with the people there. You could extend this theme further by contrasting the people from two different cultures who live alongside each other. Or you might just photograph people of around the same age, lighting them in much the same way and posing them to emphasize their common background.

The American photographer Bill Owens made a book from his collection of family portraits in a small town. Each family was photographed in their own house looking directly at the camera. He used the same camera, lens and film combination each time in order to bring out the differences between the families, while retaining the feeling that they all had something in common.

A neighbourhood can also be portrayed by concentrating on the focal points of area—the shops, cafés and restaurants, for instance, where people meet one another. You could choose to photograph one café as it reflects the neighbourhood and its activities during the course of the day. Early in the morning you might find workers from a nearby market having breakfast, and by mid morning you could see a group of

Parisian cityscape *Inner city areas often include modern developments which provide graphic pictures, especially if you can include a figure*

Water pump *To photograph the local children, it may be worth looking for subjects around popular meeting places —like this water pump*

move away, others move in. Children grow up, and the notorious kid who terrorized every cat in the street soon becomes a well-dressed young man taking his girlfriend out to the movies. These are all subjects for your camera, either with or without their knowledge. While it can be very lazy simply to take pictures out of your window, with the same background and profile view, it would be justified if you were to mount all the prints side by side, showing the range of individuals or even, in the long term, the development of a youngster. This could be a project for which you use an old camera, permanently mounted so as to give exactly the same shot each time a subject moves into view.

shoppers stopping for coffee. At lunch-time the local office workers might fill every seat, hurrying in and out before their lunch break is over, but later in the afternoon it is likely to become quiet, most customers being people with time on their hands, the retired, or possibly students whose lectures have finished. In the evening the place may assume yet another character, and in this way the mix of people that make up a neighbourhood can be illustrated.

Following on from this theme you could photograph a day in the life of an entire street, photographing perhaps with a wide angle from a single viewpoint to show the various activities that occur during a typical working day.

One of the most interesting themes which takes a different perspective on the neighbourhood is one which shows how things change over a period of time, whether it is a redevelopment scheme over a period of years, or simply the seasonal changes which alter the face of an area. On the other hand, a quaint village street which is about to be changed by the positioning of an adjacent motorway can be recorded in a series of 'before' and 'after' pictures. A careful viewpoint with a telephoto lens can make the motorway appear to be almost on top of the village, threatening its small existence.

Even on a smaller scale, such a treatment has its value. Things change everywhere, and often without warning. The old tree that has to be felled because it was struck by lightning, the distant view that is now blocked because someone built an extension to their home—all these are points to consider when taking your photographs. Bear this in mind as you look round, and try to identify such features so that you can record them while they survive.

But while much of this involves straightforward record photography, strive at all times to make the pictures good ones in their own right. When taking a view down the street, for example, do not simply stand in the middle of the road and press the button. A moderate wide angle lens will help to include some nearby objects as well as showing the view, so position yourself so as to make a mirror feature of something—a hedge, an attractive gatepost, or the framing branches of a tree perhaps. Alternatively, you might crouch right down at pavement level so that its texture serves to provide some interest rather than simply being a bland, featureless expanse in the lower half of the picture. Choose a good day with the light in the right direction and with a few clouds in the sky to provide interest in what would otherwise be another featureless area. Having selected your viewpoint and lens, you can choose the lighting conditions whenever they are just right—maybe a year will pass until you get the right combination, but you will have the satisfaction of having taken a shot in which you have exercised all your skill to make it so.

Newcastle street *This neighbourhood is juxtaposed with the city as a whole. The golden light romanticizes and softens the harsher side of the industrial scene.* **Fire alarm** *Though this object may be of little interest to locals, it is the sort of detail which the photographer can use as a strong and interesting pointer to an area's character.* **Shopkeeper** *Local figures that you know may be more than willing to pose for you in their own settings.* **Washing** *In dull or rather cheerless locations, look for bright splashes of colour to enliven your shots and break up the monochrome effect.*

The final difficulty with photographing your own neighbourhood—and for some people, perhaps the main obstacle—lies in persuading yourself that it is worth doing at all which raises questions about why one takes pictures at all, but there are several possible motivations for photographing your own neighbourhood. You can do it as an exercise in photography, with no thought of showing the pictures to other people or for exhibition. But if your pictures turn out to be particularly interesting, then you could well find that you have material of exhibition quality.

Maybe your local library or town hall would like to mount a display of them. And there is also the possibility that others will be interested—your local history society, or authors writing books about the area. As the years go by, your growing documentation of the life and people of your neighbourhood could become a unique and worthwhile record.

Monuments

Monuments are among the most photographed of subjects—so finding new ways of approaching them can be an exciting as well as difficult challenge. It helps if you know something of your subject's history

Gargoyles at Notre Dame *Unusual foreground subjects can lead the eye towards or contrast with another building of a very different nature*

Wailing Wall, Jerusalem *An attractive sky makes all the difference to the composition when the monument itself, although famous, is not beautiful*

The term 'monument' does not refer only to something ancient and grandiose —almost any notable structure great or small of local or national importance falls into this category. The very diversity of subjects that you are likely to come across, therefore, means that no single approach can be right for every occasion. In fact just how you approach photographing monuments depends on what you want from the final images.

For example, you may simply want a record shot of the postcard type as a document of, perhaps, a quick visit to a certain place. This may involve showing the monument only as the focal point in a much wider scene. On the other hand, you may take a technical approach with the intention of showing the monument as accurately and with as much detail and clarity as possible. A further alternative, and often the most exciting approach, is to try and create an interesting and unusual image which draws upon your own very personal interpretation of the subject.

Most monuments have some sort of association, either historical or personal—they may have been built in honour, or commemoration, of a person or event, or simply as a form of expression. Because of this many are designed to attract the attention and therefore tend

to be impressive or interesting enough in their own right to be worth a picture. But this basic attraction may draw the unwary photographer towards the mundane record shot. To get a more interesting picture you may find that thinking about the monument's association provides better clues to taking more interesting shots. Often, where the monument is particularly famous, you will already know why it was built and may have formed your own ideas on the subject. In such cases the idea for the picture may be preconceived or conjured up beforehand. But if you know little of the subject in hand, make a point of finding out about it before you start shooting. You may discover many new ways of approach that stem naturally from the subject and would not have occurred to you otherwise.

You can adapt your approach to suit the history of the monument. Gothic buildings, particularly cathedrals, with their tall spires and soaring arches, were often built to give the impression of man aspiring to the heavens. You can help the medieval architects by accentuating the height and grace of these buildings in your photograph. One way of doing this is to move in close to one of the spires and shoot upwards with a wide angle lens. With a vertical format to

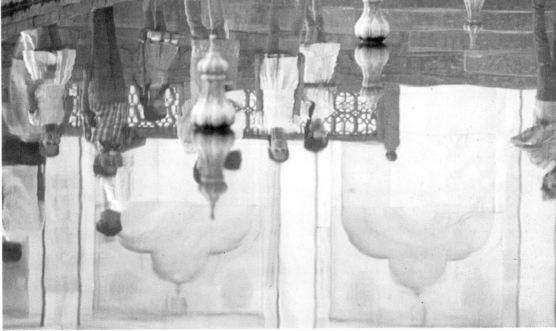

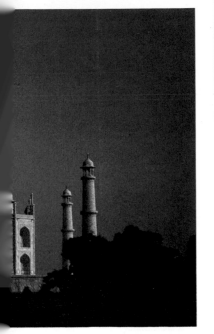

Reflection, the Taj Mahal
Reflections can give an unusual view of a well known monument while people can add a splash of colour to an otherwise dull picture
Taj Mahal *A classic view is often best for a symmetrical building like this one, while moonlight lends a romantic touch*

avoid an over-solid base, the strongly converging verticals may seem to be soaring into the heavens. This approach may be particularly effective on a cloudy overcast day when the spire seems to be almost touching the sky. But another popular approach is to shoot with the narrowest aperture possible when the sun is right above the spire at midday,

so that the spire is in silhouette and the top seems to burst with light—an effect exaggerated with a wide angle lens.

These are just a few of the approaches you can try out with Gothic buildings: there are, of course, many others. It is important to analyze just what is striking or beautiful in the monument and photograph it in such a way as to bring this out. A Moorish palace, for instance, often seems to exude a cool elegance which can sometimes be caught at its best very early on a sunny morning when the light is still slightly tinged with blue— particularly if you can include water in the shot and keep the composition very clean and simple. The most striking thing about a Greek temple, however, can often simply be the contrast with the blue sky. To show this to best effect try an almost abstract shot from a low viewpoint—perhaps with a telephoto—with the white stone of the temple shining in the midday sun contrasted against the sky. The possibilities are endless.

There is no reason why you should include the whole of the monument in your shots—very often details are more interesting than the whole. This is not only true of old buildings, but also of modern ones—some very successful shots have been taken of the tops of Art Deco skyscrapers showing the intricate pillars and window designs. You can often select details which sum up the style of the monument or the historical period which produced it—Egyptian designs or the sculpture at the tops of

columns can often convey much more than a straightforward view of a monument. By concentrating on small but significant details you can use them as symbols to create powerful moods. An old castle may well have massive stone blocks showing interesting weather-beaten textures—by taking close ups of these you could convey the impressive scale of the castle walls better than by photographing the whole castle.

The opposite approach to this is to present a monument in its context. It is generally better to choose angles that keep people out of the frame, so choose a time of day when there are few people around, or fit a dark neutral density filter to make them 'disappear' from your shot. But sometimes you need the people in the shot to give it some atmosphere. This is particularly obvious in situations where life around the monument has changed little for hundreds of years—the people can be as much a part of the monument as the structure itself. Usually though these people must be doing something positive rather than simply passing by—and they should be very obviously 'local' unless you wish to show the monument as a tourist attraction.

Often a monument contrasts strongly with its surroundings and this contrast may provide some interesting shots. For example, a rich mosque could be contrasted with the squalid hovels around it. A telephoto lens or a wide angle can both be used to do this. From

Sacre Coeur, Paris
White buildings look very effective when seen against a blue sky. A well selected view can sometimes be much more expressive than the whole structure
London Monument
With a telephoto lens you can compress space, a useful technique when you want to bring two contrasting buildings into juxtaposition
Salisbury Cathedral
A careful composition with a wide angle lens allows verticals to converge in a way that is consistent with the style of architecture
Athens at dusk *Many monuments look much more effective in semi silhouette, and the evening light is a useful way of obscuring untidy surroundings*
The Leaning Tower, Pisa
The unusual viewpoint of this famous tower not only gives a new look to the subject, but a dramatic idea of the way the tower leans over

a distance with a telephoto, the mosque can be made to appear to rise out of the mass of huts. By shooting from closer with a shorter lens, on the other hand, and including one of the huts in the foreground, you can make it appear to loom over the mosque.

Many ancient monuments in cities are surrounded by modern buildings which often tower over it and a building once regarded as grand can appear slightly ridiculous. You can emphasise this in your shot by keeping the monument small in the frame. You do not have to dwarf the monument to achieve the same effect—just by including an incongruous or very modern detail in the picture, you can emphasise how the atmosphere of

The Capitol, Washington *This stunning effect is produced simply by moving the zoom control while making a long exposure. Many buildings look much more glamorous at night, especially if they are floodlit so that they stand out against the dark sky.*

Selim Mosque in snow *Unusual weather conditions make all the difference to a building, and instead of intruding, a foreground figure adds a little local colour and atmosphere to the photograph*

the past has been destroyed by later developments. A shot of an ancient ruin reflected in the windows of a souvenir shop or a plate glass cafe in the foreground would be an example of this approach. In many countries, small plastic replicas of monuments are available—try juxtaposing the real monument with one of these.

You may not want to show the whole monument, but only a silhouette, or certain details, to give certain moods. Choose your lighting to hide or reveal certain details. If the texture of a monument—the roughness or smoothness of the stone—is attractive, shoot when the surface is illuminated by strong side lighting.

Some monuments can appear pale and colourless for most of the day, but you can use warm early morning or evening sunlight to add a colourful glow to the shot. This can be particularly effective late on a rather changeable day, when the sky behind the monument is a contrasting dull grey. Striking and unusual views can sometimes be achieved by shooting the reflection of the building in a puddle or a wet pavement. The warm light on the monument contrasts with the cold grey of the surroundings. Because so many monuments are photographed in bright sunlight, wet weather gives you

the opportunity of presenting them out of context. Reflections and glistening surfaces can be used in a variety of ways, and very often, the poorer the weather, the more interesting pictures are.

Many monuments have an air of mystery, and if you want to accentuate this, try shooting in mist. Mist hides detail but adds mood—really thick mist might reveal nothing but the battlements of a ruined castle giving it a powerful presence.

Monuments are usually presented as grandiose, but there is no reason why they should occupy the greater part of the frame. Many interesting pictures of monuments concentrate on the sky, giving an impression of great space. A dramatic skyscape can emphasize the impressive isolation of a monument, but bear in mind that a bright and featureless sky is rarely interesting. Try to choose a sky with heavy clouds. When the sky is cloudless, graduated filters can darken an uninteresting sky, while leaving the lower part of the picture brighter. By combining a graduated filter with a warming filter such as one of the 81 series, you can take effective photographs of a monument under a brooding, copper-coloured sky. However, do not overdo this type of picture, or it may be too obviously artificial.

Hardy's houses

Some buildings naturally lend themselves to producing attractive images, others don't. John Sims demonstrates how an imaginative approach can make up for any shortcomings

Often photographers are assigned to photograph places which do not at first appear to be ideal subjects. Nevertheless, they are expected to produce attractive results. And images that are effective because the photographer has worked hard to create something interesting, not because the subject itself is striking, are always difficult to achieve.

The houses lived in by the 19th century English writer Thomas Hardy are cases in point. The most famous is an attractive cottage at Upper Bockhampton, Dorset, a picturesque location photographed by thousands of tourists every year. But Hardy also had a house in London, a nondescript town house now overshadowed by a busy road and a major railway line—not the sort of place that anyone would want to photograph unless they had a specific assignment to do so. We sent John Sims to photograph both of these houses to compare the type of approach that is involved in each case.

Most people who photograph the cottage in Dorset stand inside the fence and frame their shot to include as much of the house and garden that their lenses will take in. John deliberately avoided this approach and tried several different ways of creating a more unusual interpretation of the scene.

The London house was more of a problem. Since there were cars parked in front of the house and a railway line blocking his view, John found that there was no way of obtaining a satisfactory shot at close range. However, by photographing from the top of a tall residential building nearby he managed to frame his shots to include the house, the railway line and the road, creating both an attractive picture as well as making a statement about the changes which have taken place since Hardy's day.

Town house *The only way John could take a straight shot of the house was to use a 300 mm lens from the top of a nearby block*

Country cottage *For a broad view of the cottage John waited for the afternoon light and framed the shot to lead the eye to it*

High viewpoint *Shooting from a nearby building, John used a range of lenses on his Nikon, depending on how much of the surroundings he wanted to include*

Busy neighbourhood *To show how much things have changed since Hardy's day, John deliberately included the busy surroundings. He waited for the buses to pass to add colour*

Night time *By using an exposure time of 60 seconds, John recorded the trails of car lights on his Kodachrome 64 film. 55 mm lens at f/8, and the Nikon F2S mounted on a tripod*

Cottage at night *The dusk light helped create an atmospheric study of the old building. The interior lights added to the mood of the scene. 30 second exposure, 24 mm lens at f/8*

Through the foliage *For a more unusual shot, John deliberately framed the photograph through a bush in the garden. The red blooms added colour to the muted tones and were deliberately defocused*

Window *For another successful night shot, John focused on the portraits of Hardy which were hanging inside. His Nikon F2's TTL meter gave the right exposure for the interior but John still bracketed*

From cottage to castle

Photographing architectural subjects can be very rewarding. Once you have mastered the basic problems of perspective, composition and lighting, every building offers creative potential for the photographer

Even in the smallest town there is usually an immense variety of buildings, each with its own individual character, charm and style. And as most buildings are designed to look good, many hold great potential as particularly attractive subjects.

Unfortunately, as all too many photographs show, whatever the theme, simply having an attractive subject does not automatically guarantee an attractive appealing picture. For a start, buildings are meant to be seen in three dimensions, not two, so to convey photographically something more of a building than a flat unimpressive image, a careful, thoughtful approach is needed. Given this, even the humblest crofter's cottage can make as interesting and attractive a picture as the most splendid medieval castle.

One of the most important considerations in architectural photography is that of light. Good light can literally make or break a picture. The right weather conditions and the right time of day can reveal the best in any building. The colours of brick and stone acquire their full value in sunlight, and textures and details are thrown into relief, allowing you to concentrate on those aspects of the structure which interest you most.

Different types of daylight suit different buildings and, if you have time, it is a good idea to observe buildings under various weather conditions, and at various times of the day. A few minutes either way can see one wall plunged into the deepest shadow or dramatically lit by diagonal light as the sun moves steadily around. Always be ready to take advantage of rapid changes in light. A break in the clouds can send a shaft of light across an otherwise dull cityscape, picking out buildings and giving them extra solidity. Always look for the special 'something' which conveys the atmosphere of each particular building.

Strong clear light is particularly good for bringing life to dull grey stone work.

Even the most uninteresting stone buildings can be made attractive by the warm light just before the sun goes down. Strong directional light is also good for abstract photographs of buildings and architectural details; shapes and shadows are more pronounced and can be isolated to form very attractive compositions.

Other buildings may look better in the diffused light of a slightly overcast day. A white building, or a wall that is always in shade, for instance, is better illuminated by soft light reflected from the clouds. On the other hand, a bank of heavy clouds on a wet day or the menacing appearance of a stormy sky may provide an atmospheric backdrop for Gothic buildings or castles. Wet weather is also appropriate when you want a

Silver roof *It is always worth waiting for the moment in a storm when a shaft of light suddenly illuminates a feature of a building against a dark sky*

grim shot of desolate buildings such as a large factory or rundown slums.

Under certain lighting conditions, filters can also be valuable. 81 series filters are useful for warming up the colours of stonework on an overcast day and by using a 5R filter you can add an attractive pinkish hue to an otherwise dull stone building.

A polarizing filter may help to visually separate a building from its surroundings, particularly on a sunny day, because it dramatically darkens blue skies and increases contrast. Use a polarizing filter for eliminating unpleasant reflections from modern glass buildings as well. Reflections are not the only problem when shooting in strong sunlight; extremes of contrast may also

be difficult to cope with; areas of deep black shadow may fall right next to intense highlights where the sunlight catches a white wall.

But you can use these extremes of contrast creatively. With a small building in the centre of the frame, for example, heavily shadowed by the tower blocks around it, you have to decide whether to expose for the highlights or shadows. If you want the small building to appear as a dark, barely visible shape set dramatically amongst the full brightly-lit blocks, you can expose for the highlights. Remember that most TTL meters are centre-weighted, however, and if your camera has automatic exposure it may expose for the shadow in the centre. So, with an automatic camera, you must

be prepared to use the manual override if possible.

Another problem associated with photographing buildings which can also be used creatively is the problem of converging verticals. This occurs when you point a camera upwards to include the whole of a building in the frame. The building appears to lean away from the camera: the effect becomes even more dramatic with wide angle lenses. This is because by tilting the camera you have placed the film at a different angle from that of the subject. Although the effect can be exploited creatively to produce some striking images, particularly of modern high-rise buildings, it usually spoils photographs and is best avoided.

You can avoid converging verticals by keeping the camera exactly parallel with the face of the building but you may cut off the top of the building in your photograph instead.

With a 35 mm camera, one solution is to turn the camera around to use the vertical format. However, although this may admit the top of the building into the frame, it may also include a large and perhaps uninteresting foreground, especially if you are using a wide angle lens. Frame your shot to include a tree, flowers, a group of passers-by or some other interest in the space in front of the building. The creative use of the foreground can make the final image much more arresting. But watch out for unwanted distractions in the foreground—

Temple and lotus *A wide angle lens has a great depth of field and enables you to relate foreground and background elements in a pronounced way*

Barn *Even the most mundane building can make a good picture. Try using a long focal length lens to concentrate on pattern, colour or texture*

lamp posts, parked cars, unsightly pavements or gutters.

Another way of avoiding converging verticals is to find a higher view point— perhaps another building across the road. If your new viewpoint is sufficiently far away, you may be able to use a medium telephoto to isolate the building from its surroundings or to select individual details.

Some excellent examples of how photographers cope with converging verticals are shown in the last section, *Modern Buildings*, (page 147 to page 151).

If you are planning to photograph buildings, aim to take as many lenses as you can carry easily so that you can shoot the same subject from a wide range of viewpoints. It is also worth taking a tripod because it is that much easier to compose your picture carefully with the camera in a fixed position. You will find, too, that a mounted camera decreases the temptation to 'shoot from the hip' and that you give each exposure more attention and thought.

When you are composing your shots,

Reflection *Give a new slant to photographs of buildings by looking for an unusual approach. This reflection works well*

Bow fronts *Dull skies create ideal conditions for enhancing subtle colouring. Using a telephoto lens from an angle brings out the form of these houses*

Balcony *The photographer has picked out one balcony from many similar ones on a block of flats with a telephoto lens, and made maximum use of the lines of shadow in the bright sunshine to emphasize the abstract composition*

Suburbia *A carefully chosen high viewpoint reveals the pattern made by this housing development, while the flatness of the lighting gives a quiet mood*

bear in mind that buildings are made by people and for people. Often you can create more interest and atmosphere in your photographs by including people in the frame. You may have to wait a little before the cleaner moves to exactly the right place or the people emerge after work, but it is often worth the effort.

Sometimes, however, a building can look better when people are deliberately excluded—in a shot of a grand old building, for instance, passers-by may be unpleasantly distracting. In a busy city scene, though, you may find it virtually impossible to shoot before somebody wanders into the frame. One solution is to get up very early in the morning and take your picture before anyone else is around—early morning light can also be very attractive. If you want to shoot at a busier time of day, you can use a neutral density filter that allows a long exposure, so that anyone moving does not register on the film and appear in the picture.

An area worth exploring is the relationships between buildings of different sizes and styles. Contrasts in style or size can often be emphasized by using a long focus lens because the apparent flattening of perspective brings buildings close together.

When relating a building to its surroundings, scale is important, and this can frequently be conveyed by including figures so that relative size is understood immediately by the viewer. The sheer enormity of many formal gardens, like Blenheim Palace or Versailles, can be conveyed by including a tiny human figure. Abstract geometrical patterns, like a paved courtyard can also convey a sense of space.

When you are photographing buildings in rural settings, the wide open spaces can be used to advantage but try to relate the building to its surroundings. Many thatched cottages, for example, have lovely gardens which have almost become part of the house; it would be absurd not to include at least some of the garden when photographing the house. By photographing a castle from a vantage point that includes its setting, you may be able to convey some of the impact it had in times of old. Remember too that many castles used water as a defence, and reflections from the moat can add greatly to the composition. Given a still day, and good weather conditions, you can take a photograph in which it is hard to tell the real bricks and mortar from their watery double. However, it is as well to have a polarizing filter at hand to reduce unwanted reflections if, for example, the water surface is disturbed by wind.

Try to find a good viewpoint for your subject. Sometimes the right viewpoint is immediately obvious—some

buildings positively demand to be seen from certain angles. At other times you may have to walk around for hours before you find the right approach.

On trips to little known country areas, or when travelling abroad, it is worth having a detailed road map to help to find the best vantage point. It may also help you discover remote buildings— abandoned houses, tumble-down cottages, empty farms, and crumbling castles are all excellent subjects. The sad atmosphere and the picturesque nature of decay can provide an evo-

cative and wistful photograph, particularly if you shoot early in the morning or late in the afternoon when long shadows throw fascinating patterns across the richly coloured brickwork or the weathered stone pile ruins.

If you develop an interest in architectural photography, the vast number of buildings found in any town or city means that you will never be short of subject matter. Once you have mastered problems of perspective, composition and lighting you will be rewarded with many attractive photographs.

Fog *Shooting from a taller building nearby, the photographer used the swirling fog of San Francisco to make the most of the space age nature of the tower*

Streets apart

Comparing an old print of an area with the way it looks now can make an interesting assignment and, as Homer Sykes shows, prompts a range of ideas

90 years ago *This is one of the prints that inspired Homer to document the area's modern face*

Facelift *The buildings are the same but the facades have changed. A 35 mm lens framed this symmetrical view*

Nearly a hundred years ago, before tall buildings punctuated the London skyline, before there were tedious, smoggy traffic jams, photographers were already making a record of their surroundings. As they lugged their huge wooden plate cameras and tripods across the cobbled streets, perhaps they wondered if future generations would ever see their faded prints and marvel at the way things used to be.

Indeed, many people are interested in looking at images of the past and gaining insight into the way our city streets have changed. This is what inspired Homer Sykes to photograph a small area of Battersea, London, which he had seen depicted in a series of old prints at his local library. Using these prints as a starting point, Homer set off to document the way the area has changed and to shoot a set of photographs that conveyed his own personal impressions of the area.

He was surprised to find that many streets were still recognizable and he framed his own shots to include some of the same buildings. In many cases, the only thing that had changed was the facades—a local ironmonger now a wine bar—the structures were largely original. Yet there were also immense changes — whole neighbourhoods cleared away to make room for monolithic housing complexes.

For this assignment Homer felt it was

144

important to try and cover the area from several different viewpoints—especially the ones which people come across everyday. So often photographers fail to notice potential subjects in their own territory becuase of its familiarity—they walk along a pavement or drive past in their cars and miss the very things which sum up an area. But Homer deliberately exploited these common viewpoints to create interesting photographs—even to the extent of using his camera while behind the wheel of his car.

Homer's general approach was to walk around the area at random looking out for potential subjects. When he found a detail or a facade, he chose not to photograph it straight away but to wait until an interesting figure walked into the frame. This added human interest and produced a more involved and complete statement about the area.

Tower blocks *These large buildings are featured and framed to overshadow the woman*

Young couple *Two youngsters looking for jobs? Homer felt this shot showed another modern change*

555 *The red door and street number caught Homer's eye, but the human element completes the scene*

Modern buildings

Much of modern architecture appears on the surface bland and repetitive. Yet there are many exciting modern buildings, and even the less immediately attractive examples provide a challenging and fascinating subject for the creative photographer

At first sight modern buildings may not seem a particularly inspiring subject for photography. What, after all, is interesting about the drab colours and repetitive shapes of so much modern architecture? Yet despite, and indeed largely because of, the simplicity of modern buildings, they can represent a clean canvas, providing much more scope for creative photography than more conventional architecture.

Straightforward record shots of a whole modern building or buildings taken from a distance will rarely result in exciting images. Few examples of

World Trade Centre *Framing the composition with a foreground object is all the more effective if, as here, its form echoes shapes in the main building.*
Curves *By selecting simple elements and framing tightly, you can make a very pleasing composition*

modern architecture are visually interesting enough to justify such an approach. Instead it is necessary to enliven the photo by various means. Shooting at dusk can produce good results, as can night photography. In night shots bear in mind the colour cast which

those 'white' lights will produce in the final picture. Fluorescent lighting shows up as green while the tungsten or sodium floodlighting which sometimes illuminates the building will produce a rich yellow or orange glow. It is sometimes possible to filter out these casts to a greater or lesser degree but generally speaking you should try to use the colour rather than neutralize it.

Another way to liven up distant shots is to use interesting juxtapositions—for example, shooting from a downtown area with a 1000 mm lens so that the run down Victorian areas are seen dwarfed by their newer and glossier cousins.

Juxtaposition can also be a good technique to bear in mind while shooting from closer to the subject. Rather than try to disguise the bleakness of the endless expanses of concrete and glass, emphasize it by including in the photo a small but brightly coloured foreground object. This should be carefully placed in the overall composition—putting it right in the centre will generally

produce very dull results whereas shifting it to one side or to a bottom corner will help to create a feeling of tension with the vast building pressing down on the detail. Elements as simple as a road sign or lamp post or the top of a brightly coloured bus can be very effective in this approach. As always, simplicity is the rule and it is usually best to make the picture from the two basic elements of the bright detail and the drab block. Close in until all traces of the sky and other potential distractions are removed from the frame.

While small details can help in this way to add impact to a simple abstract, they can also be used to give a different kind of picture. Try, for example, indicating the vast scale of modern buildings by including the people who work in them as a tiny element of the photograph. Photograph an enormous glossy lobby with people milling about. Shoot down the side of a building from an adjoining one and the tiny dots of people walking around outside will give a more

effective indication of scale than the featureless sky which results if you shoot up in the more conventional manner. Even the tiniest image of a person or people will be immediately recognizable, so make them deliberately small to heighten the effect.

Because of the starkness of modern buildings you can play around with all sorts of special effects and unusual angles. Simplicity is essential in these compositions—any excess of detail or other source of distraction will tend to destroy the abstract effect—so search the viewfinder carefully for these distractions before taking a shot. Often this means closing in on the building with a long lens. A zoom lens will be particularly useful for this kind of approach, allowing you to crop tightly and overcoming some of the problems which prevent you from getting to an ideal viewpoint.

Because you are looking for abstraction rather than accuracy you can shoot from many angles—indeed the distortion

Sculpture *A foreground object can often help to bring out the strengths of the main subject. Here the triangular shape of the modern sculpture, with its vivid colouring, heightens the surging energy of Paris's Tour Fiat in the background.*

Reflection *The strongly converging verticals of a shot straight up the side of a tower can be impressive—especially with a wide angle—but an extra detail, such as this reflection, may lift the shot out of the ordinary.*

Dallas *To photograph a building with an interesting shape, you should try to find a combination of viewpoint and lens which allows you to exclude any extraneous distractions, keeping the number of elements down to the absolute minimum. This lets the building speak for itself*

149

resulting from shooting from a strange angle can often be the main point of the picture. It is not always necessary to hold the camera either vertically or horizontally. Holding the camera at an angle generally produces a rather weird and unnatural effect but this may be precisely what you need for some photos.

Strong diagonal lines or long curves sweeping from corner to corner give a dynamic effect and can look particularly effective when combined with tone or colour contrasts. Here wide angle lenses giving strange perspectives can be used, particularly from very close to the building, to give these strong lines. However, if you find that the wide angle makes precise framing difficult, switch back to the zoom.

If you look only at one building you may miss interesting contrasts and comparisons. Instead, try creating interesting angles between two or more adjoining buildings or shooting one smaller building against the stark backdrop of its larger neighbour.

As they have little colour of their own, modern buildings respond well to strongly coloured filtering. Try a violet or magenta filter to create a glamorous modernistic effect (but only on cloudy, overcast days). Blue filters give a cool, hard effect. And there is now a full range of graduated filters to make a bland sky more exciting and 'hold in' the composition. On bright sunny days, a polarizing filter may be found to give the best results, darkening the sky to a richer tone. Polarizing filters, however, also affect the reflections from windows and other reflecting surfaces such as perspex, so check the image in the viewfinder to ensure that the result you are getting is the one you want.

Reflections make bad enemies but

Dwarfed *Juxtaposing old and new architecture emphasizes the contrast between the styles of two eras*

Abstract *The patterns made by stark shapes, bright colours and patches of dense shadow typical of modern buildings can make effective abstracts*

good friends. If you fail to take them into account you may find that they are merely an annoying distraction. On the other hand, using them creatively can add impact to an otherwise boring shot. Look for interesting reflections in individual windows or, for a different perspective, move right back and use the building's entire expanse of glass. For example, try moving to another building, some distance away, and photographing an individual building or whole skyline at sunset or sunrise with the sun behind you. The glasswork will reflect the sun straight back at you, making the building stand out against a dark sky.

A similar and even more dramatic effect results when a building or buildings are caught by the sun breaking briefly through a brooding overcast sky. There is a large element of luck in such shots but you can increase your 'luck' by choosing your day carefully.

The lighting at the time you take your photograph will make a great difference to the final result so forward planning is essential for good results. If you want a detailed overall shot of either the whole of the building or a section, go at a time when the sky is fairly overcast, giving soft diffused lighting. Alternatively, abstract photographs, emphasizing the strong patterns and harsh lines of modern buildings, will probably have more impact if shot in a bright sun, when the contrast between bright highlight

and dark shadow will tend to emphasize the pattern.

In addition the time of year needs to be carefully considered. Summer gives blue skies more reliably but on a crisp winter day the air can be cleaner, giving a clearer result with fewer low fluffy clouds. Winter will also have obvious effects on any foliage which appears in the picture. Some buildings will be partially obscured behind trees in the summer while autumn reveals clear lines and shapes. Other buildings, especially very recent ones, incorporate bushes,

Dusk *Sunset makes the most of an impressive skyline as the skyscrapers, with their vast expanses of glass, stand out from their surroundings in rich, glowing colours*

The human element *However small in the frame, figures inevitably catch the eye, and provide a focus for shots of the slab sides of starkly designed modern buildings which may otherwise look rather dull*

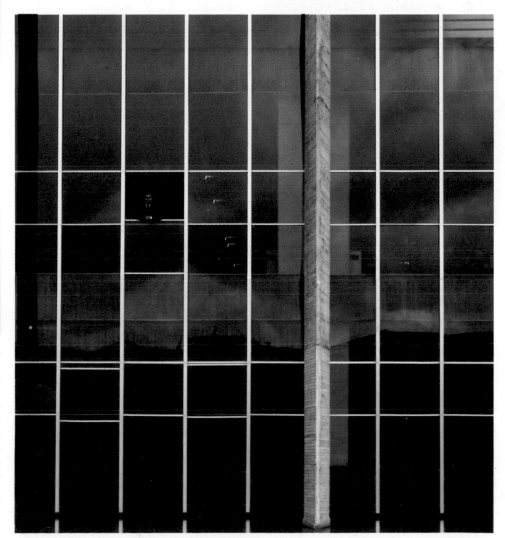

ivy or even small trees to deliberately soften the harsh uniformity of constant straight lines and these elements will appear at their best in spring or summer.

Your approach should always be 'sympathetic' to the building—you need not necessarily show it in a favourable light, but your treatment should be in keeping with its character. If the building scorns fussy detail and depends on strong, clean lines, for instance, then an equally bold, simple approach is probably most suitable. But ultimately, the choice is yours.

INDEX

Page numbers in *italics* refer to illustrations